HD 62.7 .H35 1991

Halloran, James W.

Why entrepreneurs fail

Why
Entrepreneurs
Fail

You Mustn't Quit

When things go wrong, as they sometimes will,
When the road you're trudging seems all uphill,
When the funds are low and the debts are high
And you want to smile, but you have to sigh,
When care is pressing you down a bit,
Rest! if you must—but never quit.

Life is queer, with its twist and turns,
As everyone of us sometimes learns,
And many a failure turns about
When he might have won if he'd stuck it out;
Stick to your task, though the pace seems slow—
You may succeed with one more blow.

Success is failure turned inside out—
The silver tint of the clouds of doubt—
And you never can tell how close you are,
It may be near when it seems afar;
So stick to the fight when you're hardest hit—
It's when things seem worst that you mustn't quit.

(Author Unknown)

Why Entrepreneurs Fail

Avoid the 20 Fatal Pitfalls of Running Your Business

James W. Halloran

LIBERTY HALL
PRESS™

LIBERTY HALL PRESS books are published by LIBERTY HALL PRESS an imprint of McGraw-Hill, Inc. Its trademark, consisting of the words "LIBERTY HALL PRESS" and the portrayal of Benjamin Franklin, is registered in the United States Patent and Trademark Office.

FIRST EDITION
FIRST PRINTING

© 1991 by LIBERTY HALL PRESS, an imprint of McGraw-Hill, Inc.

Printed in the United States of America. All rights reserved. The publisher takes no responsibility for the use of any of the materials or methods described in this book, nor for the products thereof.

Library of Congress Cataloging-in-Publication Data

Halloran, James W.
Why entrepreneurs fail : avoid the 20 fatal pitfalls of running your business / by James W. Halloran.
p.   cm.
Includes index.
ISBN 0-8306-3511-4 (pbk.)
1. Small business—Management.   I. Title.
HD62.7.H35 1990
658.4'21—dc20   90-43823
                                                  CIP

For information about other McGraw-Hill materials, call 1-800-2-MCGRAW in the U.S. In other countries call your nearest McGraw-Hill office.

Questions regarding the content of this book should be addressed to:

Reader Inquiry Branch
LIBERTY HALL PRESS
Blue Ridge Summit, PA 17294-0850

Vice President and Editorial Director: David J. Conti
Technical Editor: Lori Flaherty
Production: Katherine G. Brown
Book Design: Jaclyn J. Boone

Contents

Dedication
In memory of my friend the late George R. Horton,
a reminder of the virtue of gentleness

Acknowledgments
My great appreciation is extended to Lorrie Burroughs
and Deborah Sommers of the SBDC Connection at the
University of Georgia for their help in assembling the
bibliography of reference materials. Thanks to Jim
Watkins for his input on financial planning and to Hen-
rietta Cowan for her assistance and patience.

Introduction

AS A SMALL BUSINESS OWNER, CONSULTANT, AND TEACHER FOR THE PAST 17 YEARS, I AM constantly asked, "What is the biggest problem for the small business owner?" Invariably the questioner wants a one- or two-word answer such as "undercapitalization," or "lack of experience," while I, on the other hand, would like to sit down for hours and explain the whole picture. Because I can't usually do that, I have put together the most common stumbling blocks that businesses fall prey to in *Why Entrepreneurs Fail: Avoid the 20 Fatal Pitfalls of Running Your Business*. The small business owner who can circumvent the 20 problem areas in this book can, I assure you, succeed in all their business endeavors.

As you proceed through the book, you will meet a host of characters who have encountered problems that are very familiar to all small business owners. Meet Woody, who chose a business that is incompatible with his background and interests.

Bill, a dropout successful corporate executive, finds that what he expects and what he receives from buying a business are totally different. Then there is Sally, who learns the hard way the requirements for choosing a successful location.

Paula, a small manufacturer, doesn't plan for cash flow fluctuations and cuts herself short of funds while Ben discovers he's chosen the wrong company structure and loses money by forfeiting his personal tax deductions.

Herb learns that personally designing his advertising program pays big dividends, then George instills a new sales philosophy that backfires.

Roger learns his payroll expenses are escalating as his turnover increases because of his inconsistent management.

Larry, whose ego gets in the way of properly planning an expansion of his business, gets burned. Finally, Joe, a manufacturer, learns he can't quit because he hasn't planned for retirement.

You will witness the problems of these business owners and learn what could have been done to avoid the "fatal" mistake. Each story is followed with realistic advice as to how these pitfalls can be avoided. This book is your opportunity to learn from the mistakes of others.

At the conclusion of each story and solution, you will find a guideline or exercise to follow to help you from falling victim to the pitfall. These reminders should be kept within easy reach as you operate your business.

There is also an up-to-date bibliography of recent publications available for your reference library. The listings, grouped by subject, are books published since 1986 and should be available through your bookstore or direct order from the publishers. Approximately 200 titles are included. It is important for you to pursue all available educational channels in your pursuit for entrepreneurial success. Arming yourself with the knowledge and strategies from those entrepreneurs who have walked the same path is invaluable.

The characters you will meet in the stories are real, as are the scenarios, only the names have been changed. The characters are, in most cases, victims of circumstance, not victims of stupidity. They are typical small business owners who are so busy directing their businesses that they are not always able to keep up with all that is around them. The 20 fatal pitfalls will always be there, but with some forethought and planning, you can avoid them. By reading this book, you will be forewarned and reminded of the dangers that await to assail you.

Pitfall 1

Choosing an incompatible business

Opening a business with little consideration to personal satisfaction

WOODY HARMON HAD SPENT HIS ENTIRE 22-YEAR CAREER AS AN AIRLINE PILOT FOR A major commercial airline. Labor and management problems threatened to close the airline in 1989. He was too old to be considered a young hotshot who could easily catch on with another airline and too young to consider retirement. Woody knew he must prepare for a new career if the company collapsed. It didn't take long. He developed a friendship with Bob Sinclair, the owner of a local yogurt store chain. "Great business, great profit potential, Woody, as long as you work hard and keep an eye on it." It sounded perfect to Woody. He spent a Saturday helping Bob at one of the stores and excitedly reported to his wife, Ann, that he had found what he wanted to do. Ann worried about Woody's lack of business experience, but Woody was insistent that it was right for him. She kept her fingers crossed that the airline would continue to fly.

It didn't, and Woody signed a three-year lease within two weeks of his job's demise. He borrowed $75,000 on his house, and, with Bob's help and advice, ordered all the equipment and yogurt mix needed to open the store.

Sixty days later, Woody was the unhappiest he had ever been. He absolutely hated the yogurt business. Working seven days a week, confined to a 1,200 square foot store, and supervising sales clerks was as far from what he was used to as he could get. Business had started slowly, further depressing him. He was making poor business decisions, was irritable at home, and couldn't sleep thinking of his large, sinking investment. He looked to the sky with every passing airplane. Why, he thought, did he ever think he could be a retailer. He belonged in aviation, not in a shopping center.

Taking the advice of his friends and his wife, he put the store up for sale. His goal was to get out. Priced at the $75,000 he invested, he found a buyer within a month. The terms were not great, $10,000 down and the rest over five years. The buyer was a divorced woman in need of a career. Six months into the agreement she backed out. Business was weak and she was remarrying and moving out of state. "It's all yours, Woody. You will have to take it back. By the way, I am three months late on rent." Now Woody was in worse shape. The landlord would claim the property if rent was not paid, so Woody wrote a check for $4,500 and was back in the yogurt business. What made it worse was that he had gotten back into aviation as the manager of an avionics supply business at the airport and was totally enjoying this new experience of helping private pilots. He feared he would have to leave this new position to protect his investment by working in the business he had grown to hate. In desperation, he called Bob Sinclair and offered him the business for whatever he considered fair. Luckily for Woody, Bob gave a reasonable settlement. Although much of the investment was lost, Woody was finally out from under and able to work in the environment best suited for him.

Matching compatability to pursuit

A panic decision to open a business in an unfamiliar environment is a sure ticket to failure. Woody fell victim to this. His decision was impulsive and his plan was non existent. He left an environment that had become part of him for one that was totally foreign to him.

Losing a job can often be the worse scenario for opening a new business. The potential owner has just gone through an exhausting psychological experience and is not prepared to make the necessary and difficult decisions in an objective manner. Woody grabbed at the first straw. If he had taken his time and given thoughtful analysis to what his true needs were he would have chosen an area of compatibility. In the end, he found that area in the avionics supply business. It is too bad he was not able to identify that earlier before losing money and time pursuing the ill-fated yogurt store. Hopefully, he will rebound in the future and possibly be able to invest in a business opportunity in the aviation industry.

I wish Woody would have been more open to the advice and suggestions of friends and his spouse. He refused to listen because he was afraid to hear the limitations. Small business owners need a support group to explore their ideas with. If you can't get support, particularly from family, it might be a fatal flaw. Because owning a business is so engrossing, it is not fair to your family to proceed without their support. You will need their understanding and involvement if you expect to realize your goals.

Woody's other critical mistake was acting impulsively without a business plan. It is imperative that the entrepreneur write out a plan to guide him. It serves as a map and a reference resource. How to write a plan and what should be addressed in it is discussed in chapter 3.

The starting point of finding a compatible business is doing a personal analysis of yourself. This requires looking at your past in making decisions regarding your future. The goal is to find the environment that makes you feel good and fulfilled. A two-step process of recognizing past events in your career that were rewarding and identifying the personal values that you hold dear can help you find an environment that will allow you to reach your goals. If you are considering a full-time occupation as a small business owner, you will most likely spend, at least initially, 50, 60, or 70 hours per week in this pursuit. It will become part of you. If it is right, it will be fulfilling and exciting. If it doesn't fit, you will regret the day you opened the door.

There are professional career-testing devices (available through career testing centers) that can help you with this exercise. I believe you can achieve the same objective, however, by following these steps:

1. Thoughtfully analyze your career up to this point, and make a list of events that have been meaningful to you. They don't necessarily have to be great milestones, maybe completing a certain project, coming up with a brilliant idea, or smoothing over some personnel problems at your workplace come to mind. The list will be longer than you think and might look similar to the one shown in Table 1–1.

   Analyze what characteristics of yours that were being put to use at the time of these incidents. Was it your creative instincts? The technical aspects of a job that allowed you to show your expertise? Or maybe it was using managerial capabilities of assuming responsibilities and working through people. The idea is to identify what abilities you enjoy using the most and feel personally good utilizing.

   Study it for a pattern of what type of activity has been important to you to feel accomplishment. It may or may not be what you are used to doing.

_____ Table 1–1. _____
Rewarding work incidents

When	What	Why
Jan. '83	opened the Wilson account	they said it couldn't be done
summer '83	company picnic	invited to eat with the boss
Jan. '84	named sales rookie of the year	recognition
fall '84	became a sales trainer	added responsibility
early '85	intervened with credit not to close Parker Bros	helped Harry Parker from losing his store
Jan. '86	became regional manager	more money, prestige
fall '86	got Jan a promotion	helped Jan
'87	talked Joe into adding territory	new challenge
summer '87	won family trip to Hawaii	fun for my family
December '87	solved conflict with Bill and Jerry	relieved tension
March '88	straightened out McFadden account	saved major account

We sometimes presume that just because we are good at doing something it must be right. That is a very limited mind-set because it relates to circumstance more than to personal fulfillment.

2. List the personal values you hold most dear. You can't successfully do anything that conflicts with these. Table 1–2 lists some values to choose from, you might include others. This list should not exceed the ten that are most important to you.

3. By combining both lists into a T-chart you will be able to analyze essential contributors to what makes you happy at work. The happier you are with your work, the better you'll be able to work closer to your potential as a human being. Figure 1-1 is an example of how you can analyze your list for a potential business venture. If you're successful, you will have matched your values and your attitudes to give you insight into what type of opportunities you should pursue.

4. There is another personal analysis you need to do. This is the time to check your pulse to make sure you have the necessary resolve and resilience to

Table 1–2.

Personal values checklist

_____ Achievement (sense of accomplishment/promotion)

_____ Adventure (exploration, risks, excitement)

_____ Authenticity (being frank and genuinely yourself)

_____ Enjoyment (from doing my work/enjoying it)

_____ Expertness (being good at something important)

_____ Family (happy and contented living situation; having time with my family)

_____ Friendship (working with people I like and to be liked by them)

_____ Independence (acting in terms of my own schedule and priorities; making own choice)

_____ Intellect (having a keen, active mind)

_____ Leadership (having influence and authority)

_____ Location (able to live where I want)

_____ Loyalty (being loyal to my boss and the organization and to have loyalty in return)

_____ Meaningful work (relevant and purposeful job)

_____ Money (having plenty of money for the things I want)

_____ Physical health (attractiveness and vitality)

_____ Prestige (being seen as successful; recognition for contributions)

_____ Security (having a secure and stable position)

_____ Self-growth (continuing exploration and development)

_____ Service (contributing to satisfaction of others)

_____ Spirituality (meaning to life; religious beliefs)

handle the pursuit. The business world is not for the lighthearted or casual observer. To be successful, you must possess the personal characteristics of confidence, determination, and creativity.

Incident	Value correlation
opened Wilson account	achievement
company picnic	prestige, loyalty
rookie of the year	achievement, expertness
sales trainer	achievement, expertness
saved Parker Bros.	achievement, service
regional manager	achievement, prestige, leadership
helped Jan	service, achievement
new territory	adventure, self growth
family trip	family, enjoyment
resolved conflict	friendship
McFadden account	achievement, expertness service

Fig. 1–1. A T-chart such as this one can help you analyze the essential contributors to what makes you happy at work.

Personal characteristics for success

Probably the most important characteristic an entrepreneur must have is confidence, because there will be days when everything will go wrong. The confident entrepreneur will go to bed on these nights with the attitude that tomorrow will be a better day. You will also need confidence to be an effective decision maker. As a small business owner, there is no buck passing. You will make, and be responsible for, all decisions. They will not always be right so there must be the built in confidence that the next decision will be the right one.

Determination is what will motivate you to reach the light at the end of the tunnel, however. No matter how good your idea or how good your management, it will take time to accomplish your goal. Determination to succeed will allow you to cross over any obstacles in your path.

Creativity is what will separate you from the competition. The business that does things a little better than the competition eventually wins if all else is equal. Doing that little extra will get the attention of the customer. This takes creativity as well as hard work.

Therefore, take the time to analyze your confidence level in your idea, your determination to succeed, and your plan for creatively outdoing the competition before proceeding.

5. Recognize your financial needs and abilities—how much money is available for a business venture and how much money must be made from it. This goal-setting exercise is discussed in more detail in chapter 2, but, for now,

_____ **Table 1–3.** _____

Net worth calculation

Assets		Liabilities	
Cash on hand	$_____	Notes payable to bank	$_____
Government securities	$_____	Notes payable to others	$_____
Stocks and/or bonds	$_____	Accounts and bills due	$_____
Accounts and notes		Real estate mortgage	
receivable	$_____	Home	$_____
Real estate owned		Other	$_____
Home	$_____	Other debts	$_____
Other	$_____		$_____
Automobile(s)	$_____		$_____
Cash surrender value -			
life insurance	$_____		$_____
Other assets	$_____		
		Total liabilities	$_____
Total assets	$_____		

Net worth calculation:

Total assets		$_____
Total liabilities		$_____
Net Worth (total assets		
less liabilities)		$_____
Available for business investment		$_____

My objective is to become an entrepreneur by establishing a _____ business. As such, I will be able to control my own destiny and be responsible for the profits and losses of my business. By doing this, I will gain recognition from my family and my community for the work and contributions that I perform. It will enable me to better reach my potential in my personal and professional career. My long-term objective is to develop a substantial business entity with the potential of building appreciable equity that I can sell, pass on to family members at my retirement, or continue as an owner on an absentee management basis.

My immediate financial objective is to meet my essential income needs and ensure myself of an eventual return on my investment. To accomplish this, I must receive a minimum income of $_____ per year initially with a strong potential of increasing my income to $6.6. within a _____ year period of time. In order to achieve this goal, I am willing to invest $_____ of my personal assets in the operation. The business _____ (name) will open no later than _____, 19__ .

Fig. 1–2. Write a mission statement that you can later use to weigh business opportunities with.

complete Table 1–3. You need to address financial limitations and capabilities to have realistic expectations about the environment you desire.

6. Conclude this exercise by writing a mission statement. This two-paragraph statement should be your reference point in making all future decisions regarding opportunities. Paragraph one should address your personal objectives and paragraph two your financial objectives. See the example in Figure 1–2.

Pitfall #1 summary
career questionnaire

The following questionnaire is designed to help you select the working environment that best suits you. By analyzing why you have made certain decisions in your career, and what career incidents brought you the greatest satisfaction, you would get a good idea of the general direction you should pursue in finding a compatible business.

1. What are your greatest working aspirations?
2. What type of changes in your job responsibilities do you enjoy the most?
3. How would you describe your work career?
4. When have you particularly enjoyed your job?
5. What characteristics of your career have been most important to you?
6. When do you dislike your work?
7. When is it important for you to receive recognition?
8. When do you feel the most fulfillment from your work?
9. If you could, what would you change about your job?
10. Do you feel the goals of your organization stimulate the individuals employed?

Pitfall 2

Unrealistic expectations
The hassled executive who drops out to own a business

"I'LL TELL YOU JERRY, I HAVE PAID THE PRICE FOR SUCCESS." BILL LANKFORD WAS collaborating over drinks with his best friend. "I am a CEO for a large company, I have never had so much money, and I am too exhausted to enjoy it. Except for weekends, I have been home three nights in the past month. That's a typical month. I feel I have lost touch with my family. My job has turned into a PR job—all I do is travel and make speeches. Success is great for the ego, but what about the soul? I envy you owning your own small business and being able to control your own timetable. I don't need the money as much as I need to slow down. That's why I called you. I want your opinion on a business opportunity. It's a chain of six laundromats here in the metro area. It sounds ideal to me. Take a look at this statement." (See Table 2–1.)

Jerry reviewed the statement that showed a business that turned an $80,000 profit before the owner's salary. The selling price was $150,000. Bill had figured that he could cut his present salary to $50,000 and allow a $30,000 payback on the investment to equal a 20 percent return. "I really want it, Jerry. I would not have to travel. I would spend part of each day at home in my office and the other part out checking on the locations. It seems ideal. Each store has its own manager, so if I want to take a trip with the family or play golf, I will be free to do so. I can open additional outlets to generate more profits. I will be able to control my own destiny, have independence, and make good profits. No more corporate world. What do you think, should I write the man a check?"

Jerry was scratching his head in consternation. "Bill, I think you need to slow it down a bit. I don't think it is quite the scenario you are expecting. Believe me, I have

_____ **Table 2–1.** _____

Laundromats income statement

Revenues	$239,770
Operating Expenses	
Payroll	$56,000
Rent	37,600
Maintenance and Repairs	21,230
Supplies	11,450
Utilities	9,980
Advertising	2,300
Accounting and legal	1,750
Insurance	1,950
Payroll taxes and licenses	3,150
Depreciation	6,700
Miscellaneous	8,600
Total Operating expense	$160,410
Net Profit before taxes	$79,360

owned a business for 16 years, and it's harder than you think. I don't know the laundromat business, but I can guarantee you there will be some unexpected surprises."

"Aw, come on Jerry, this is a piece of cake compared to what I have been involved with. You are just spoiled. I am going to do it."

The company was shocked at Bill's resignation. There were goodbye parties, gifts, and a genuine display of sorrow. Bill was deeply touched and had, at times, some fleeting second thoughts.

Jerry proved to be right. What Bill expected and what he received were far different. It was not a "piece of cake." The maintenance of equipment alone was a nightmare. He spent many afternoons surrounded by pieces of washing and drying machines. In addition, the store managers were constantly asking for more wages or quitting on a moment's notice. He did not realize that controlling an expense budget of $160,000 could prove just as vexing as one of $12,000,000. Every added expense was a subtraction from his already decreased salary. His first attempt at opening an additional outlet was a shock. He had not realized it took at least 18 months to build a profitable base. It was another drain on his cash flow.

Worst of all, he missed his old company. He missed being treated and looked upon as a CEO. The travel, the speeches, the people, the fast pace had become part of his routine and he missed them. Even the promised utopia of his return to family was less than expected. Too many evenings were ruined because of his restlessness and irritability. He was afraid to leave the business for any extended trips. The headaches of the new job were just as tiring as the old ones.

"Why," thought Bill, "couldn't I have just better controlled and balanced my previous job. After all, I was the CEO, but I was so convinced of greener pastures."

Preliminary business evaluation

Greener pastures—always greener pastures. We all fall victim to this syndrome in certain areas of our lives. Bill Lankford certainly did in reaching his decision. The very nature of small business ownership is depicted as an "American dream," adding to the greener pastures idealism. Dreams of success must be tempered, however, with a realistic look at what an opportunity really represents. Bill saw in the opportunity only what he wanted to see. He refused to listen to Jerry. He did not want his dream to be interrupted. He totally overlooked some of the things that were important to him. His exhaustion with his job situation caused him to consider an escape mechanism. He should have first:

1. Taken some time away from work to consider what was missing. There are bound to be times of fatigue while working on a career path. Being tired is often confused with "burn out," which implies no longer having the desire or ability to pursue a career path. Taking a retreat might open your eyes to being tired, not "burned out."

2. Taken steps to fill the void of corporate life. As noted, particularly in Bill's case as a CEO, he might have been able to eliminate or alter the objectionable parts of his job in order to make it agreeable. Possibly delegating the speeches to his vice president and reducing the amount of his travel would have given him fresh insight into his position.

3. Discussed at length with Jerry the pitfalls of small business ownership. A detailed interrogation of Jerry's career path would have been enlightening and given him some realistic expectations.

4. Read books and attended seminars on small business ownership. There must always be an educational stage for any career. Bill skipped this step. There are many courses available through community colleges and government agencies that can help fill this void. Libraries and bookstores are also good resources.

5. Spent time working on-site with the previous owner of the laundromats before making the decision to buy. This opportunity was certainly available to Bill and would have given him great insight into what he was headed for.

Building expectations with no experience has caused Bill to make a very regrettable decision.

Establishing personal needs

Don't enter an industry totally cold. Take the time to learn the environment by working in it. Spend Saturdays, evenings, or vacation time becoming part of the industry. The best way to enter an industry is on a part-time basis while continuing full-time employment. In many pursuits, you can get started by starting ownership on a small basis and building on the base until the market demands that you be there full time. In the preceding case, Bill could have considered buying one outlet at a time and allowing it to operate under his part-time supervision until he felt comfortable with future expectations. After you have received enough exposure and taken some basic educational steps such as reading and/or attending classes, you will be able to establish criteria for making an informed decision. These criteria include income and life-style goals and your tolerance for risk.

Income goals

The income you need to make initially, and what you expect to make eventually, is based on the information you have collected about the business and the amount of money you have invested. You must be absolutely sure these goals are a reality. Don't stretch the figures to meet these goals, and don't underestimate your needs. You will still have house payments, food costs, insurance, and utility bills that must be met. You positively cannot consider an opportunity that does not meet your basic, immediate needs. It takes time to build a solid profit base, and you will probably have to make sacrifices. If your idea is good, and you are willing to work hard, you can eventually reach your projected profit level but it requires patience and persistence in getting to that point. Therefore, income expectations should be as conservative as possible.

Life-style goals

Will your expectations of your life-style be met? Retailers do not just stand behind cash registers smiling, they also unload trucks, clean up stockrooms, and move fixtures. Manufacturers spend very little of their time at trade shows or closing big deals, they also pack cartons, argue with suppliers, and administer to personnel. Restaurant owners do more than greet customers. If the cook, a waitress, or a dishwasher do not show up for work, guess what? Consequently, you need to think about the things you might be unwilling to accept. Start by listing your expectations about ownership using the following guidelines.

1. Analyze your personal needs hierarchy. Dr. Abraham Maslow's Hierarchy of Needs theory states that we have five levels of personal needs. The lowest two needs, psychological (water, food) and safety (shelter, warmth), are consistent in all of us—We must have them met. The three higher needs of belonging, self-esteem, and self-actualization, vary greatly among us. It is more important to some than to others to belong to organizations or family. To some, self-esteem, or status, needs are very important to achieve. Others have a greater need to feel fulfilled, self-actualization, in what they do for a career. It is important to discover whether your intended pursuit can meet your own expectations of personal needs.

2. The hours you expect to work, including at-home time as well. Seldom does the small business owner have the luxury of being able to leave his work at the office. You and your family must recognize the extent of the time involved.

3. The physical effort involved. Have you considered any physical limitations you might have such as a bad back or split shins. You will probably not have the luxury, at least initially, to hire stockroom help or a maintenance staff.

More than likely, you'll have to do some manual labor so make sure you are able.

4. The travel required, including trade shows, client visitations, and educational seminars or meetings. If you are considering a small business because you are tired of the travel in your present occupation, make sure your new venture agrees with this expectation.

5. The extent of community involvement deemed advisable. Many types of businesses benefit greatly from associations with the chamber of commerce, rotary clubs, auxiliary clubs, etc. To some people, this type of PR work is unacceptable. If you fit that description, be aware of this possibility.

6. The type of work you think you will be doing the majority of the time you are at work, i.e., sales, clerical, working with your hands. Sometimes, what you view from the outside about the duties of a particular type of business owner can be very misleading in how they really spend their time. Show this list to someone involved with the industry you are considering and listen for their feedback.

Your risk tolerance

How much of a risk are you willing to assume? In order to aim for a high profit level, an entrepreneur needs to expect a high degree of risk. Usually, the lower the risk, the lower the profit potential. Being one of the first to try a new idea means exploring unknown frontiers that means more risk. Following a proven formula, such as an established franchise, cuts down on the risk by reducing the uncertainty. It also requires more investment and limits the profit ceiling. We all handle risk differently so identify your risk tolerance and make sure it can handle the opportunity.

Pitfall #2 summary
assessment questionnaire

The following questions are designed to stimulate your ideas about your career goals and your own personal expectations of business ownership. Answer the questions sincerely.

1. What is your minimum income requirements for the first year of your business or expansion?

2. What is your anticipated income level after three years of this business activity?

3. What personal satisfaction do you expect to receive from this endeavor?

4. Will you receive a feeling of self esteem from this pursuit?

5. What type of work activity will you be spending the majority of your time doing as a result of this decision?

6. How much direct contact will you have with people? Is this level of interpersonal contact acceptable?

7. How many hours per week are you willing to devote to this business?

8. How much travel do you envision?

9. What hours of the day will you be active in this business?

10. How much entertainment of customers will be required? How much will you be entertained?

11. Will joining community or industry organizations be beneficial to this business? If so, how much involvement with these groups is acceptable to you?

12. Do you have the physical and psychological capabilities to handle this challenge?

13. Presuming you can borrow equal to what money you can invest, do you have the financial capability of entering this market?

14. How do you rate the risk factor? Is it acceptable to you and your family?

Pitfall 3

Using a business plan not tailored to you

An entrepreneur relies on a business plan that is not his own

JIM ANSEL WAS FEELING ANXIOUS AS HE WAITED TO SEE MR. BOYD, A VICE PRESIDENT with First National Bank. He had carefully considered what he was going to say in regards to his $20,000 loan request to start an electronics service company. He had brought with him some notes he had put together to support the request.

Mr. Boyd came in and assumed the chair behind his desk. "So Jim, you wanted to see me about a loan to start a business. Let's start by looking at your business plan and go from there."

"I don't have anything really written out Mr. Boyd, just some rough notes, but I have formulated in my mind what I am going to do," stammered Jim. "Do I need to write it out?"

"Of course you do Jim, I can't take your thoughts to the loan committee. I need a written description that includes the financial projections, market analysis, and all other pertinent information that will allow us to make a decision. Write up your notes and any other thoughts and come back to see me when you are ready."

Jim felt foolish as he left the bank. He should have known it wouldn't be that easy. Now he had to write a business plan and he didn't know how to start. He decided he had better visit an accounting or consulting firm for some help.

He took his notes to a business planning service the next day. It was easier than he thought, although much more expensive than he had envisioned. He had a short interview with a consultant and presented him with his projections and his cost estimates. One day later, a nice looking computer printout was ready along with a bill for $800. It certainly looked impressive, and although Jim did not thoroughly understand the figures, the profit projections were even higher than what he had estimated. He rushed it over to Mr. Boyd.

"Jim this is a nice looking document but you have not validated any of the figures. You can't just say you are going to do $50,000 in sales without telling us how. I need your input on your market, not just a computer compilation of figures. This looks like a report for how electronics service businesses do generally in the industry. I know this is what you hope, but is it the truth for your market? We need to know about Jim Ansel's business in particular. I cannot get a loan approval on this type of plan."

Ingredients of a good business plan

Jim's laziness has caused him to get duped. What he bought was an impressive report from a computer on how electronic services should do. It was a programmed report with little or no regard for Jim's abilities, location, or marketing ability. A computer cannot write a business plan. It can only spill out historical ratios of previous like businesses. You will need to write the plan and it will only be as effective as the information you gather to put into it. Whether it is a new business or an expansion of a present business, you need to write a business plan that is uniquely tailored to your particular situation. In its original form, it does need to follow a particular format. It is first and foremost a personal guide for you to follow. It can be formalized for financing purposes at a later date. A good business plan must include the following 13 ingredients.

1. A mission statement. This is your purpose, your goals, and your hopes. It can be as simple as three short paragraphs:

    Paragraph one states your personal objectives. Why are you doing this besides the idea of making money. What makes it so important that you are willing to take the risk involved. Is it an opportunity to use under-utilized abilities, a chance to make a special contribution to society, an opportunity to express yourself? There must be strong motivation towards some type of personal satisfaction if it is going to succeed.

    Paragraph two states your financial objective. In consideration of how much money and time you are going to invest, what do you realistically expect to receive from the venture. Address at least two segments of time, the first year and then the third and maybe the fifth year. Keep in mind the hazards and growing pains of initial growth during the first year and you should keep your objectives minimal, however, by the end of the third or fifth year some of your plans should bear fruit.

    Paragraph three sets the timetable. If you are serious about this, it is time to set a date. This will serve as a motivation to get on with it. Give yourself plenty of time, because a good idea needs time to develop. Initially, this can be just a projected starting date. Eventually, however, you can develop it into a complete chronological listing of all activities to be done before opening, as shown in Fig. 3–1.

2. "For sale" market investigation. Whether or not you have any interest in buying an existing business, if there is an opportunity available for sale, take the time to investigate it. It is a very educational process. You will gain

New Store Checklist	
To Do	Deadline before
Select store location	16 weeks
Select lawyer and accountant	16 weeks
Sign lease	16 weeks
Prepare floor plan-measure site	16 weeks
Plan dollar stock investment by resources	12 weeks
Purchase floor covering, wall paper, etc.	12 weeks
Plan store hours	12 weeks
Order cash register	12 weeks
Prepare stock control system	10 weeks
Order wrapping supplies, store stationery	10 weeks
Order pricing tickets	10 weeks
Place merchandise orders with resources	10 weeks
Plan bookkeeping system	8 weeks
Select store manager	8 weeks
Plan grand opening promotion	8 weeks
Conduct store management training program	8 weeks
Secure insurance	8 weeks
Notify utilities	4 weeks
Secure licenses	4 weeks
Buy fire extinguishers	4 weeks
Order cleaning equipment	4 weeks
Buy tools and stepladder	4 weeks
Order office equipment	4 weeks
Secure forms, job applications, W-4's, etc.	4 weeks
Make merchandising signs	4 weeks
Hire sales People	2 weeks
Install telephone	2 weeks
Install shelving in stockroom	2 weeks
Install carpeting, wallpaper, paint	2 weeks
Prepare customer request book	2 weeks
Secure sales tax charts	2 weeks
Buy supplies	2 weeks
Open bank account	2 weeks
Receive and price merchandise	1 week
Set up fixtures and merchandise	1 week
Set up weekly schedule for salespeople	1 week
Place advertising for grand opening	1 week

Fig. 3–1. Store checklist.

tremendous exposure to the market by looking at someone else's business. You will also gain immediate access to a possible competitor's position. You will learn the relative market value of a similar business, and you might even end up finding a good opportunity.

3. Location and market analysis. This step requires considerable research. Start with a total demographic study of the market area you are considering. A complete demographic study will include population statistics, per capita income figures, educational levels of the population, race ratios, unemployment levels, and even a breakdown of sales in the area by classification. Check with your local library, chamber of commerce, closest college or university, or any large commercial developers for this type of information. It might require inquiries to government agencies such as the state sales tax division to put it all together.

   Analyzing location sites also requires an extensive collection of information. Once possible alternatives are identified, you should spend whatever time necessary taking traffic counts of pedestrian walk-bys or car drive-bys. Check with the state department of transportation for automobile traffic counts at key intersections.

4. The organization structure. You will need to decide if you should be a sole proprietorship, partnership, or corporation. Learn the advantages and disadvantages of each. You might want to check with an accountant, consultant, or attorney before making this decision.

5. A financing plan. Although financial projections are initially just an estimate, as you collect more information, it becomes more concrete. Use a form such as the one shown in Fig. 3–2 and do it in pencil until the final plan is put together.

6. Identify the target market. Label very specifically who your ideal customer will be. This will a detailed description of the type of individuals or companies you know you can sell to. For individuals, it will include age, education, sex, income level, and interests. For companies, it will include size, purpose, and needs. The target market is what decides your marketing approach, location decision, and your physical design. These are the customers you must please.

7. A marketing plan. How will you attract and sell to customers? Describe your advertising and sales philosophy. Identify the most appropriate media to use, project a budget, and show a calendar of advertising and sales promotion dates. Explain the sales methods you and your sales staff will employ. How will you train sales people? How will you pay them?

8. A pricing strategy. Develop a pricing strategy that includes the following:
   ~The cost of the product
   ~Operation and all overhead expenses
   ~Profit
   ~Retained earnings to be used for the continued growth and expansion of the business.

9. A cash flow plan. All businesses have cycles of fluctuating income due to seasons, deliveries, or sales strategy. Income must be tracked on a monthly basis to make sure the owner is prepared for these cycles. The business plan should show the amount of projected available cash at the beginning of each month.

Start-up business plan

Item	Estimated monthly expense COL I	X	Months = COL II	Total year's expense COL I × 12
Owner's Salary		3		
Other Salary		3		
*Rent		3		
Advertising		3		
Supplies		3		
Telephone-Utilities		3		
Accounting		3		
Insurance		3		
Loan Principal and Interest		3		
Taxes		3		
Miscellaneous		3		
Total month expense				← Total Year Expense

Starting cost paid only once

	Start-up expenses
Fixtures and equipment	
Decorating—remodeling	
Installation cost	
Starting inventory	
Utility deposits	
Legal fees and others	
Opening promotion	
Cash on hand	
Other	
TOTAL PAID ONLY ONCE EXP.	

Start-up capital

Start-up expense $_____
Only once exp. $_____
Total cash needed $_____

1st Year Income & Expense

Total retail sales $_____
Cost of sales 50% $_____
Gross profit $_____
Total year expense
    $_____
Total Only Once
    $_____ $_____
Net profit $_____

*Figuring Rent:
Store is 20 ft × 70 ft = 1400 sq. ft. Rent is charged by the square foot. If the rent is $10 per sq. ft. per year, 1400 sq. ft. × $10 per sq. ft. = $14,000 per year. $14,000 per year ÷ 12 = $1166.67 per month.

Fig. 3–2. Financial planning form.

10. Pro forma (projected) income statements and balance sheets. These are the financial statements that show the projected profit and worth of the business. This should include a minimum of two years of projections.

11. An inventory plan. How much inventory is needed to reach the projections and when and how will it be purchased? This is a purchase plan. Its purpose is to ensure an orderly flow of materials and products into the business so that sales will not be interrupted because of unavailable goods.

12. A personnel plan. How many employees are needed to operate the business efficiently? What are the skills needed? Where will they come from? How much will they be paid? What benefits will you be able to offer? Who will report to who? Show an organization chart and include a job description of the different positions.

13. An insurance plan. This is an area that is often overlooked and comes as a big surprise. The insurance industry has become extremely complex and unpredictable. You will need to learn how it applies to your situation before proceeding. Find an agent who knows the industry. A good agent knows how to write policies that can save the business owner money. Be careful not to underinsure, however. The expense of covering a very likely risk will be well worth the money.

As you proceed through the lessons these thirteen points will be illustrated and explained in detail. The business plan questionnaire at the conclusion of this lesson is designed to stimulate the information collection process.

How to write a business plan

Once you have written out a plan to your satisfaction, you will be able to adapt various versions of it for interested parties. The original is the most complete, however, and serves as your guide. Some excerpts of it, or all of it, can be used for securing financing. Once you've decided what should be included, formalize it, and type it up for presentation. Appendix A shows an example of a formal business plan and loan request.

Cover sheet

Name of Business, names of principals, address, and phone number of business (or owner, if start-up).

The business

A. Description of the business

B. The market

C. The competition

D. Location of the business

E. Management

F. Personnel

G. Application and expected effect of loan or investment

Financial data

A. Sources and applications of funding

B. Capital equipment list

C. Proforma cash flows
   ~Three-year summary
   ~Detail by month, first year
   ~Detail by quarter, second and third years

D. Proforma balance sheets
   ~Three-year summary
   ~Detail by month, first year
   ~Detail by quarter, second and third years

E. Proforma income statements (profit and loss statements)
   ~Three-year summary
   ~Detail by month, first year
   ~Detail by quarter, second and third years

F. Breakeven analysis

G. For an existing business
   ~Income statements for past three years
   ~Balance sheets for past three years
   ~Tax returns for past three years

Supporting Documents

Personal resumes, job descriptions, personal financial statements, credit reports, letters of reference, letters of intent, copies of leases, contracts, legal documents, and anything else of relevance to the plan.

Generally explain

1. What the business is (or will be).

2. What market you intend to service, the size of the market, and your expected share.

3. Why you can service that market better than your competition.

4. Why you have chosen your particular location.

5. What management and other personnel are required and available for the operation.

6. Why your investment or someone else's money (debt/equity) will make your business profitable.

7. What will happen to the employees.

8. What will happen to key managers.

Questions

1. Type of business: primarily retail, wholesale, manufacturing, or service?

2. What is the nature of the product(s) or service(s)?

3. Status of business: start-up, expansion of a going concern, take over of an existing business?

4. Business form: sole proprietorship, partnership, corporation?

5. Who are the customers?

6. Why is your business going to be profitable?

7. When will (did) your business open?

8. What hours of the day and days of the week will you (are you) in operation?

For a new business

1. Why will *you* be successful in this business?

2. What is *your* experience in this type of business?

3. Have you spoken with other people in *this* type of business? What was their response?

4. What will be special about your business?

5. Have you spoken with prospective trade suppliers to find out what managerial and/or technical help they will provide?

6. Have you asked about trade credit?

7. If you will be doing any contract work, what are the terms? Reference any firm contract and include it as a supporting document.

8. Do you have letters of intent for prospective suppliers of purchases?

For a takeover

1. When and by whom was the business founded?

2. Why is the owner selling it?

3. How did you arrive at a purchase price for the business?

4. What is the trend of sales?

5. If the business is going downhill, why: How can *you* turn it around?

6. How will *your* management make the business more profitable?

Generally explain who needs your product or service and why.

Questions

1. Who exactly is your market? Describe characteristics: age, sex, profession, income etc., of your various market segments.

2. What is the present size of the market?

3. What percent of the market will you have?

4. What is the market's growth potential?

5. As the market grows, does your share increase or decrease?

6. How are you going to satisfy your market?

7. How will you *attract* and *keep* this market?

8. How can you expand your market?

9. How are you going to *price* your service, product or merchandise to make a fair profit and, at the same time, be competitive?

10. What price do you anticipate getting for your product?

11. Is the price competitive?

12. Why will someone pay your price?

13. How did you arrive at the price? Is it profitable?

14. What special advantages do you offer that may justify a higher price (you don't necessarily have to engage in direct price competition).

15. Will you offer credit to your customers (accounts receivable)? If so, is this really necessary? Can you *afford* to extend credit? Can you afford bad debts?

The competition

Generally explain who your competitors are, their positions in the industry, and how your business will stack up.

Questions

1. Who are your five nearest competitors? List them by name.

2. How will your operation be better than theirs?

3. How is their business: steady? increasing? decreasing? Why?

4. How are their operations similar *and* dissimilar to yours?

5. What are their strengths and weaknesses?

6. What have you learned from watching their operations?

7. How do you plan to keep an eye on the competition?

Location of the business

Outline the terms of the sale or lease for your property and the strategic advantages you might have over another competitor.

Questions

1. What is your business address?

2. What are the physical features of your building?

3. Is your building leased or owned? State the terms.

4. If renovations are needed, what are they and the expected cost? Get quotes **in writing** from more than one contractor and include as supporting documents.

5. What is the neighborhood like (stable, changing, improving, deteriorating)?

6. Does the zoning permit your type of business?

7. What type of businesses are currently in the area?

8. Have you considered other areas? Why is *this* one the desirable site for your business?

9. How does this location affect your operating costs?

Management

Explain in detail how you will manage the business. Be sure to use your past experiences as a boon to your successful management.

Questions

1. What is your business background?

2. What management experience have you had?

3. What education have you had (both formal and informal learning experiences) that have a bearing on your managerial abilities?

4. Personal data: age, where you live and have lived, special abilities and interests, reasons for going into business.

5. Are you physically suited to the job: Stamina is important.

6. Why are *you* going to be successful at *this* venture?

7. Do you have direct operational experience in *this type of business?*

8. Do you have managerial experience in *this type of business*?

9. Do you have managerial experience acquired elsewhere—whether in totally different types of businesses, or as an offshoot of club or team membership, civic or church work, etc.?

10. Include the above information on *all* the members of your management team.

11. Who does that? Who reports to whom? Where do final decisions get made?

12. What will management be paid?

13. What other resources will be available (accountant, lawyer)?

Note: A personal financial statement must be included as a supporting document in your plan if it is a proposal for financing. Include your resume as a supporting document.

Personnel

Questions

1. What are your personnel needs now? In the near future? In five years?
2. What skills must they have?
3. Are the people you need available?
4. Will your employees be full or part-time?
5. Will you pay salaries or hourly wages?
6. Will you provide fringe benefits? If so, what? Have you calculated the cost of these fringe benefits?
7. Will you utilize overtime?
8. Will you have to train people? If so, at what cost to the business?

Application and expected effect of loan or investment

Questions

1. How much capital will your business require? How much will be your personal investment?
2. How is the loan or investment to be spent? (This can be fairly general—working capital, new equipment, inventory, supplies.)
3. What is the specific model name and/or number of your purchase(s)?
4. Who is the supplier?
5. What is the price?
6. How much will you pay in sales tax, installation charges, freight fees?
7. How will the loan or investment make your business *more* profitable?

Pitfall 4

Using inaccurate sales forecast

A retail store expands into a new product line using inaccurate information

"WHY NOT?" THOUGHT PHYLLIS. "A FINE CHINA DEPARTMENT WOULD ADD A GREAT new look and help our summer doldrums by selling to newlyweds." There was not a china shop in the town. The only china retailers in town were a jeweler and a florist. China customers had to travel to a fashion department store 30 miles away if they wanted more selection. Phyllis was sure that a complete department in her 4500 square foot gift shop could out sell the local competition.

Bill Whitehead, the sales representative for Windsor China, was very encouraging. He showed Phyllis sales figures (of smaller stores in smaller towns) that were quite impressive. A plan was drawn up to open a 600 square foot department that would sell Wedgwood fine and everyday china, silver plated and stainless steel flatware, and appropriate accessories that were targeted at the newlywed market. It would be a dramatic presentation with chandeliers, off-white plush carpet, and eloquent wallpaper. The objective was to create a complete boutique effect.

In deciding on a sales projection Phyllis, used the historical data of the rest of the store. Because the store was averaging sales of $100 per square foot of retail sales space, her estimate was $60,000 (600 sq. ft. × $100) for the first year. She reviewed this estimate with Bill who thought it was very much in line.

She also went on a fact-finding mission to a department store 200 miles away. She spent a day with a friend who worked in the china department learning how the store operated its department and its bridal registry service. A discussion with the department manager supported her confidence that she could easily reach her sales objective.

Phyllis worked with Bill on drawing up the initial inventory purchase to supply a $60,000 volume operation. The opening investment was $12,000 in china and display samples and $5,000 in flatware and accessories. This was a higher ratio of inventory to sales than the rest of her store, but she was insistent that it be a complete look.

The initial customer response was gratifying. Comments such as "how beautiful," "we needed something like this in our town," and "I'll be back," were very common. But it never caught on. One year later Phyllis liquidated the inventory. Sales were only 25 percent of her projected sales. She wondered what she had done wrong.

Collecting the proper information

Phyllis listened for what she wanted to hear. The information she did use was prejudiced to her hopes. Her information sources, Bill Whitehead, the department store manager, and the historical data from dissimilar merchandise sales, were biased, not related, to china sales in a gift-shop environment. Her downfall was not objectively researching information on her own. A proper search would have included:

1. Comparisons of gift stores, not china shops or department stores, for expected sales per square foot averages.
2. Demographic (population) information that included the age, education, and per capita income level of the local market.
3. A historical record of the number of marriage licenses applied for in the community.
4. A close look at the competition—the jeweler and the florist—for an understanding of why the customer shopped at these stores.

If she had followed these steps, she would have learned that her market was already served. The demographic study would have shown that the local population was aging dramatically, meaning that young people were not finding employment in the area and were leaving. This would have been further supported by noticing a decline in marriage licenses over the past five years.

An understanding of the competition would have been enlightening. Phyllis would have discovered that the first place a potential bride and groom go is to a jewelry store for rings and the second is very likely the florist. Gift shops are not a priority visit, therefore, her competition was getting the first chance. She also failed to appreciate the strength of the department store 30 miles away. A major purchase such as china will warrant the inconvenience of a short trip. The department store was also able to offer payment plans that were more suitable to a young couples budget than her store.

There might have been other reasons such as service policies, prices, etc., that were inhibitors, but the point is that right from the beginning, there was reason to not proceed if she had taken some basic research steps.

Projecting realistic sales

Projecting sales with no historical data is risky at best. Effective decision making is a result of careful collection and analysis of information. The more information, the less risk. It is your responsibility to spend the time to accumulate the proper information to make a reasonable projection of future probabilities.

After gathering the demographic statistics, turn to the industry for assistance. Good companies will provide good information. They can tell you how much the average customer will spend on their classification of product in a year. You can then find out, as shown in Table 4–1, how much is spent on the product per year in your community or market for comparison.

For example, if you were investigating opening a jewelry store, you might find that the average jewelry sales per capita for your market is $48. Using round figures, if your market served a population of 100,000, this would indicate jewelry sales of $4,800,000 in the past year. If you calculated the total number of jewelry outlets to be 24, divide $4,800,000 by 24 and receive an average outlet sales volume of $200,000. By taking into consideration that some of those outlets were department stores, small costume jewelry vendors, and some other stores that were not strictly jewelry outlets, you could assume that your main competition was doing higher than that average figure. If you compare the $48 average per capita to other surrounding communities' sales, you might find that it is higher or lower. Also, check with industry sources to find the national and regional average dollars spent on jewelry. You will gain an indication of how your market buys jewelry. If $48 is lower than the industry average and the surrounding communities' average, than unless there is an economic problem in the community, your market is buying jewelry out of its marketplace. Obviously it is an underserved market that needs additional or better jewelry outlets. You might be able to project that sales would increase to a $50 average per capita with a better retail market. Discounting some of the retail outlets as not direct competition, you could figure that $5,000,000 should be sold among the 10 complete retailers, or approximately $500,000 per store. Your decision can then be

Table 4–1.
Annual industry sales potential

Store Type	Total Sales	Per Capita Sales
Grocery	$1,038,734,000	$926.16
Department	74,311,000	496.08
Restaurants	58,377,000	389.71
Drug	27,562,000	184.00
Apparel	27,354,000	182.61
Furniture	13,465,000	89.89
Convenience	12,548,000	83.77
Liquor	10,719,000	71.56
Variety	6,380,000	42.59
Catalog	6,714,000	44.82
Shoe	6,138,000	40.98
Appliance	5,087,000	33.96
Jewelry	7,148,000	47.42

based on your confidence that you will be able to gain a 10 percent share of the market.

Methods like this are not sure-proof vehicles for establishing a completely accurate sales forecast, however, they are ways of using information (to build your business plan) as opposed to guessing.

Pitfall #4 summary
Where to go for information

The following is a list of private and government resources small business owners can contact for guidance, assistance, and training. Of particular interest is the listing of trade associations. These industry sources are usually your most important source of information.

Private sector resources
Small business organizations

American Entrepreneurs Association
2311 Pontius Ave.
Los Angeles, CA 90064
(213)478-0437

Chamber of Commerce of the U.S.
1615 H St., N.W., Washington, DC 20062
(202)659-6000

National Association of Development
   Companies (NADC)
1730 Rhode Island Ave. N.W.,
   Suite 209
Washington, DC 20036
(202)785-8484

National Association of Entrepreneurs
8735 Sheridan Blvd.
Westminister, CO 80003
(303)440-3322

National Association of Manufacturers
   (NAM)
1331 Pennsylvania Ave., N.W.,
   Suite 1500
Washington, DC 20004
(202)637-3046

National Association of Small Business
   Investment Companies (NASBIC)
1156 15th St., N.W., Suite 1101
Washington, DC 20005
(202)833-8230

National Association of Women
   Business Owners (NAWBO)
600 South Federal St.
Chicago, IL 60605
(312)346-2330

National Federation of Independent
   Business
150 West 20th Ave.
San Mateo, CA 94403
(415)341-7441
600 Maryland Ave., S.W., Suite 700
Washington, DC 20024
(202)554-9000

National Small Business United (NSBU)
69 Hickory Dr.
Waltham, MA 02154
(617)890-9070
1155 15th St., N.W. Suite 710
Washington, DC 20005
(202)293-8830

The Small Business Association
of New England (SBANE)
(800)368-6803
(617)890-9070

The Smaller Manufacturers
Council (SMC)
(412)391-1622

Independent Business Association
of Wisconsin (IBA)
(608)251-5546

Council of Smaller Enterprise
(COSE)
(216)621-3300

Small Business Association of
Michigan (SBAM)
(616)342-2400

Texas Small Business United
(512)366-0099

Independent Business Association
of Illinois (IBAIL)
(312)692-7306

Ohio Small Business Council
(OSBC)
(614)228-4201

Selected minority small business organizations

National Association of Investment
Companies (NAIC)
915 15th St., N.W., Suite 700
Washington, DC 20005
(202)347-8600

National Association of Black and
Minority Chambers of Commerce
654 13 St.
Oakland, CA 94612-1241
(415)451-9231

National Association of Black Women
Entrepreneurs
Box 1375
Detroit, MI 48231
(313)341-7400

National Association of Minority
Contractors
806 15th St., N.W., Suite 340
Washington, DC 20005
(202)347-8259

National Business League (NBL)
4324 Georgia Ave., N.W.
Washington, DC 20011
(202)829-5900

U.S. Hispanic Chamber of Commerce
4900 Main St., Suite 700
Kansas City, MO 64112
(816)531-6363

Selected small business-related trade associations

American Bankers Association
Washington, DC
(202)663-5000

American Council of Life Insurance
Washington, DC
(202)624-2000

American Electronics Association
Santa Clara, CA
(408)987-4200

American Farm Bureau Federation
Park Ridge, IL
(312)399-5700

American Financial Services
   Association
Washington, DC
(202)289-0400

American Health Care Association
Washington, DC
(202)833-2050

American Hotel and Motel
   Association
New York, NY
(212)265-4506

American Institute of Certified Public
   Accountants
New York, NY
(212)575-6200

American Insurance Association
New York, NY
(212)669-0400

American Retail Federation
Washington, DC
(202)783-7971

American Society of Association
   Executives
Washington, DC
(202)626-2723

American Society of Travel Agents
Washington, DC
(202)965-7520

American Trucking Association
Alexandria, VA
(703)838-1800

Associated Builders and Contractors
Washington, DC
(202)637-8800

Associated General Contractors
Washington, DC
(202)393-2040

Association of American Publishers
New York, NY
(212)689-8920

Association of Data Processing Service
   Organizations
Arlington, VA
(703)522-5055

Automotive Service Industry
   Association
Chicago, IL
(312)836-1300

Computer & Business Equipment
   Manufacturers Association
Washington, DC
(202)737-8888

Electronics Industry Association
Washington, DC
(202)457-4900

Food Marketing Institute
Washington, DC
(202)452-8444

Grocery Manufacturers Association
Washington, DC
(202)337-9400

Health Industry Distributors
   Association
Washington, DC
(202)857-1166

Health Industry Manufacturers
   Association
Washington, DC
(202)452-8242

Independent Insurance Agents of
   America
New York, NY
(212)285-4250

Independent Petroleum Association of
America
Washington, DC
(202)857-4722

Information Industry Association
Washington, DC
(202)639-8260

International Communications
Industries Association
Fairfax, VA
(703)273-7200

National Association of Broadcasters
Washington, DC
(202)429-5300

National Association of Chain Drug
Stores
Alexandria, VA
(703)549-3001

National Association of Convenience
Stores
Alexandria, VA
(703)684-3600

National Association of Home Builders
Washington, DC
(202)822-0200

National Association of Realtors
Chicago, IL
(312)329-8200

National Association of Truck Stop
Operators
Alexandria, VA
(703)549-2100

National Association of Wholesaler
Distributors
Washington, DC
(202)872-0885

National Automobile Dealers
Association
McLean, VA
(703)821-7000

National Business Incubation
Association
Carlisle, PA
(717)249-4508

National Forest Products Association
Washington, DC
(202)463-2700

National Home Furnishings Association
Chicago, IL
(312)595-0200

National Industrial Transportation
League
Washington, DC
(202)842-3870

National Lumber and Building
Materials Dealers Association
Washington, DC
(202)547-2230

National Restaurant Association
Washington, DC
(202)638-6100

Printing Industries of America
Arlington, VA
(703)841-8100

If the industry, organization, or association you are looking for is not listed, the American Society of Association Executives, located in Washington, DC, might be able to help you. The telephone number of ASAE is: (202)626-2723.

Federal assistance
Small Business Administration
1441 L St., N.W.
Washington, DC 20416
(800) 368-5855
(202) 653-7561

The Small Business Administration (SBA) is the primary source of assistance for small businesses and serves as the advocate of small business interests within the federal government. The fundamental purposes of the SBA is to aid, counsel, assist, and protect the interests of small businesses; ensure that small businesses receive a fair portion of government purchases, contracts, and subcontracts, as well as the sales of government property; make loans to small businesses concerns, state and local development companies, and the victims of floods of other catastrophes, or of certain types of economic injury; and license, regulate, and make loans to small business investment companies.

Office of Business Development
(202)653-6542

The Office of Business Development cosponsors courses and conferences, prepares informational leaflets and booklets, and encourages research into the management problems of small business concerns. It counsels and conducts workshops and courses for established, as well as prospective, businesspersons, and enlists through SCORE the volunteer aid of retired and active executives to assist small businesses in overcoming their management problems. It contracts with college and university schools of business for counseling services and training by qualified students. It counsels interested small firms on the major aspects of international trade and works with other public and private sector organizations to generate export activity and opportunities for small business manufacturers.

Companies interested in participating in joint projects with the SBA, such as Pacific Bell Directory's participation in this publication, can do so through the Office of Private Sector Initiatives.

SCORE
(800)368-5855

A majority of small businesses fail because of managerial problems. Because of this, SCORE (Service Corps of Retired Executives), was established to utilize the management skills of more than 12,000 active and retired business executives who volunteer their expertise to provide counseling and training assistance to small business. SCORE counseling services, in such areas as accounting, management assistance, and financial counseling, are provided free of charge.

These volunteers work in cooperation with the Office of Business Development's professional staff to develop the managerial skills and the economic growth of the small business community. Their services are offered not only from SBA district office locations, but also from satellite locations, usually placed in strategic business concentrations throughout each state.

SCORE has continued to expand the number of small businesses counseled and has increased the depth and scope of the counseling. Approximately 130,000 current and prospective business owners received one-on-one counseling in fiscal year 1986. In addition, SCORE is particularly active in the training of prospective owners and managers of small businesses. Approximately 136,000 received SCORE training in fiscal year 1986.

Office of Women's Business Ownership
(202)653-8000

The Office of Women's Business Ownership, a part of the SBA's Office of Business Development, was formed to implement a policy to support women entrepreneurs. The office is responsible for ensuring that the provisions of Executive Order 12138 and other administration and congressional guidance concerning women's business ownership are carried out. The primary functions of the Office of Women's Business Ownership are to:

- develop and coordinate a national program to increase the number and success of women-owned businesses while making maximum use of existing government and private sector resources;
- develop policy, plans, operating procedures and standards to effectively strengthen and improve SBA responsiveness to the needs of current or potential women business owners;
- research and evaluate the special programmatic needs of current and potential women business owners and develop and test ways of meeting them;
- provide support to the Interagency Committee on Women's Business Enterprise in fulfilling its mandate to promote, coordinate, and monitor federal efforts on behalf of women business owners;
- work with federal, state, and local governments to ensure that they consider women's business ownership in their program areas, establishing a free flow of information in both directions; and
- serve as principal liasion with business, educational, philanthropic, organizational, and community resources to assist the growth and development of women-owned business.

Minority Small Business and Capital Ownership
Development Program
(202)653-6407

The Minority Small Business and Capital Ownership Development Program was established to promote and facilitate equal access for socially and economically disadvantaged individuals to participate in the small business sector of the economy.

It is the policy of the SBA to afford minority and disadvantaged persons the opportunity to participate in the small business sector and to use all Agency resources and other private, federal, state and local assistance programs to this end. The section 8(a) Program authorizes the SBA to:

- enter into contracts with other government departments and agencies (including, but not limited to, supply services, construction, and research and development); and
- negotiate subscontracts for the performance of small business concerns owned and controlled by socially and economically disadvantaged individuals.

To be eligible for 8(a) program participation, a small business concern must be at least 51 percent owned, controlled, and daily operated by one or more socially and economically disadvantaged persons.

Socially disadvantaged individuals are those who have been subjected to racial or ethnic prejudice or cultural bias because of their identification as members of certain groups. Economically disadvantaged individuals are those socially disadvantaged individuals whose ability to compete in the free enterprise system has been impaired due to diminished capital and credit opportunities.

Black Americans, Native Americans, Hispanic Americans, Asian Pacific Americans and Asian Indian Americans have been officially designated socially disadvantaged. Members of other groups must show proof of social disadvantage. Economic disadvantage must be established for all applicants. The SBA determines eligibility on a case-by-case basis.

Section 7(j) of the Small Business Act authorizes SBA to initiate, organize, and maintain management counseling services for small disadvantaged firms. Under this authority, the SBA places grants, agreements and contracts with individuals and organizations to furnish management and technical aid to eligible businesses.

Office of Veterans Affairs
(202)653-8220

The Office of Veterans Affairs was established in 1982 within the Office of the Chief Counsel for Advocacy. It has the responsibility for providing advice and counsel to SBA management on all legislative, regulatory, economic, and management policies affecting the interests of entrepreneurs. The office is also responsible for reviewing SBA programs and the activities of other departments and agencies whose policies and regulations affect the interests of veterans in business.

In each SBA regional and district office there is a veterans affairs officer who is readily accessible to veterans seeking assistance. In accordance with Public Law 93-237, veterans are accorded "special consideration" by the SBA. Specifically, financial assistance regulations provide that qualified veterans receive higher priority in the processing and funding of loan applications. Particular attention is accorded to handicapped and Vietnam-era veterans.

International Trade Office
(202)653-7794

The International Trade Office of SBA is charged with encouraging and supporting small business' efforts to sell U.S. products and services in foreign markets. Efforts are concentrated in export counseling, financing and training, as well as establishing links with international trade organizations.

Counseling and training on international trade is provided by SBA district offices through SCORE/ACE programs and other SBA-supported counseling resources, such as Small Business Development Centers and Small Business Institutes.

The Export Information System, based on information from the United Nations, provides data on 60 of the largest importing markets. Included in the information are the 25 best product markets for U.S. exporters, trends within those markets, and major sources of foreign competition. These reports are available through SBA district offices.

Office of Procurement Assistance (202)653-6635

The SBA's Office of Procurement Assistance is responsible for ensuring that small businesses obtain a fair share of government contracts and subcontracts. SBA works closely with federal agencies and the nation's leading contractors to carry out its responsibilities through a number of programs, including: Prime Contracting; Subcontracting; Procurement Automated Source System (PASS); Certificates of Competency; and Natural Resources. Information is provided free of charge on topics to assist small businesses in selling to the U.S. government. Topics include:

- Government buying methods
- Specification, materials allocation, delivery and supplier problems
- Getting on bidders' lists
- Preparing bids and proposals
- Counsel on bidder's rights and obligations, appeal procedures, and termination and default actions
- Contractual and financial administration
- Advice on size criteria

Office of Advocacy (202)653-6808

In 1976, Congress created the Office of Advocacy to study the roll of small business in the American economy and to work for policies and programs that will create a healthier environment for small business. To this end, the office works closely with small business owners, trade associations, Congress, and the federal regulatory agencies in an effort to improve the climate for entrepreneurship, innovation, and economic growth. Its main functions are to:

- Examine the role of small business in the American economy with regard to competition, innovation, productivity, and entrepreneurship.
- Measure the impact of federal regulation and taxation on small entities and make policy recommendations that might enhance the performance of small business.

- Evaluate the credit needs of small businesses, particularly with regard to the free flow of capital to minority and women-owned enterprises.

- Serve as a conduit through which suggestions and policy criticisms are received.

- Inform the small business community of issues that affect it, and assist the entrepreneur with questions and problems regarding federal laws, regulations, and assistance programs.

Financial assistance
(202)653-6470

The SBA has two types of financial assistance programs: guaranty loans and direct loans. Most SBA loans are guaranty loans, which are made by private lenders (usually banks) and are guaranteed up to 90 percent by the SBA. While the SBA can guarantee private sector loans of up to $500,000, loans in excess of $155,000 can only be guaranteed to a maximum of 85 percent. The guaranty loan process is as follows:

1. A small business submits the loan application to an SBA-approved private lender.

2. The lender makes an initial review and, if approved for submission to the SBA, forwards the application and analysis to the local SBA office.

3. If approved by the SBA, the lender closes the loan and disburses the funds.

SBA direct loans are available only to applicants unable to secure an SBA-guaranteed loan and are limited to a maximum of $150,000. Before applying, an applicant must first seek financing from his/her bank of account and, in cities of 200,000 or more, from at least one other lender. Direct loans funds are very limited and at times are available only to certain categories of borrowers such as businesses located in high-unemployment areas, or owned by low-income individuals, handicapped individuals, Vietnam-era veterans or disabled veterans.

Applying for a business loan/SBA assistance

The following steps show you how to apply for a business loan and/or SBA assistance:

1. Prepare a current business balance sheet listing all assets, liabilities, and net worth. New business applicants should prepare an estimated balance sheet as of the day the business starts. The amount that you and/or others have to invest in the business must be stated.

2. Income (profit and loss) statements should be submitted for the current period and for the most recent three fiscal years, if available. New business applicants should prepare a detailed projection of earnings and expenses for at least the first year of operation (a monthly cash flow is recommended).

3. Prepare a current, personal financial statement of the proprietor, or each partner or stockholder owning 20 percent or more of the corporate stock in the business.

4. List collateral to be offered as security for the loan along with an estimate of the present market value of each item as well as the balance of any existing liens.

5. State the amount of the loan requested and purposes for which it is to be used.

6. Take this material to your lender. If the lender is unable or unwilling to (directly) provide the financing, the possibility of using the SBA guaranty program should be explored. The lender should be encouraged to contact the nearest SBA field office if additional program information is needed. An SBA direct loan may be possible for creditworthy applicants who are unable to obtain a guaranty loan, depending on the availability of funds. Contact the nearest SBA filed office for advice on the possibilities of a direct loan.

Small Business Innovation Research Program

The Small Business Innovation Research (SBIR) Program was established in 1982 under the Small Business Innovation Development Act. While the SBIR solicitation process and award authority was assigned to participating federal agencies, the legislation authorizes SBA to:

- Implement the program government-side.
- Set the governing program policy.
- Monitor the performance of the federal agencies participating in the program.
- Analyze the annual reports of each of these agencies on the progress of the SBIR program.
- Report SBA findings to Congress.

The functions required of SBA under the Act are implemented through the Office of Innovation, Research and Technology. Specifically, the Act requires each federal agency having an extramural research and development budget in excess of $100 million per fiscal year to establish an SBIR Program. The program is funded by setting aside a graduated percentage of research and development dollars specified by the legislation. The maximum level is 1.25 percent. The SBIR Program is a competitive award system consisting of three phases:

1. The majority of Phase I awards are $50,000 for a six-month period or less and are designed to evaluate the scientific and technical merit and feasibility of an idea.

2. In Phase II, projects from Phase I with the most potential are funded for two years to proceed with product development. The majority of these awards are funded for $500,000 or less.

3. In Phase III, private investment is involved and aimed to bring an innovation to the marketplace. This phase might also involve production contracts with a federal agency for future use by the federal government. No SBIR funds can be utilized during Phase III.

Pitfall 5

Locating on the wrong side of the street

Competing businesses on different sides of the street

SALLY WATKINS HAD WANTED A GIFT SHOP LOCATION ON POSH ST. GEORGE'S AVENUE ever since moving to the area seven years ago. The tree-lined shopping area was four blocks of the most unusual collection of boutiques one could imagine. Gift shops, ladies' fashion boutiques, unique jewelry shops, crafts, European restaurants—a dazzling collection to please the most discriminating shopper. The area was so successful that rarely did an opening appear for a new store. When a vacancy did occur, the leasing agent would check a waiting list for interested tenants.

When Sally learned that the old movie theater was to be converted into a three-story shopping complex for small stores she contacted the developer immediately.

The basic plan called for 18 store spaces, approximately 800 square feet each. The developer was hoping for a balanced tenant mix of specialty retail products and food services. The idea was to place a restaurant, a gift shop, an apparel store, and three other complementary stores on each level. This would assure a proper traffic flow throughout the complex. Sally leased the ground floor gift shop location, right inside the entranceway, a sure winner. (See Fig. 5–1.) She had carefully scrutinized the gift shops across the street and was very pleased that they all seemed to be enjoying great success.

The nine months it took to convert the theater was long enough for Sally to plan a most exciting presentation. She traveled to the leading merchandise marts for buying and consulted with top professionals on store layout. The final presentation was truly a fine store. It had the latest in fixture design, eloquent color coordinated decor, and a sophisticated cashier system.

The Theatre Shopping Galleria opened with great fanfare. Fifteen of the eighteen spaces opened on time and the initial acceptance was quite enthusiastic. Sally was very pleased with the initial 10 days receipts and the compliments seemed never-ending. After 30 days, however, she started having some concerns. The origi-

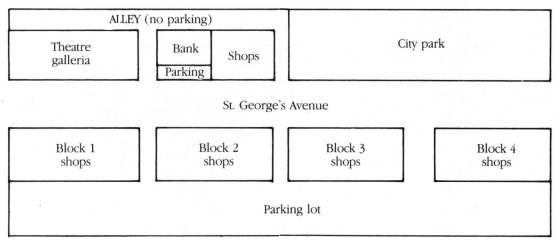

Fig. 5–1. Layout of St. George's Avenue shopping area.

nal curiosity of the shopping crowd started to thin and was not being replaced with a consistent, everyday type of traffic. Sales were very inconsistent. Some days were so hectic she couldn't keep up, others were so slow it seemed a barricade had been placed in front of the entranceway. Having gotten to know the gift merchants across the street, she was not pleased to learn that their business had returned to the brisk, consistent level they had experienced before the Theatre opening.

A year after opening, Sally was contemplating closing up. Already six of the original merchants had moved out. Even though four had been replaced, the new tenants were not of the quality or stature of the initial stores. Meanwhile, business on the other side of St. George's Avenue continued to prosper.

Location analysis

There is nothing so important to the contemporary American consumer as accessibility. This spoiled creature does not care to cross a street, find a parking place, or, in some instances, push open a door. Sally found this out the hard way. A close look at the shopping diagram shows what appeared as a minor problem being the cause for all her problems—the parking is located on the other side of the street. Except for a few places immediately in front of the theatre, a customer must walk past the competition and cross a busy street to shop at Sally's store. This is asking too much of our friend the consumer.

Another consideration that Sally failed to take into account is that we are creatures of habit. We become accustomed to our shopping habits and resist change. It takes a long time to change these habits on a regular basis, more than the year Sally has given. Notice how much attention a new restaurant receives with all the curiosity seekers. Then look six weeks later and you will find that many of those new diners returned to their old favorite eatery. This is one reason you often hear that it takes three to five years to develop a stable business—it takes that long to change a buyer's habits.

The only action Sally can take is to launch a very expensive offense. She will have to give a lot of reason for someone to cross the street. This might mean heavy advertising, price discounts, and major promotions.

You are certainly aware of the warning of being in the right place at the right time. Regardless of your business activity, location is of paramount importance. A manufacturer must be close to his suppliers and accessible to transportation methods for his customer. The same holds true for the wholesaler. Often, the business that can deliver the goods the fastest, least expensive way, will get the contract. For the retailer and service merchandiser, the more impulsive the product, the more important a convenient location is. There are many products that, if not at the most convenient location, are doomed to failure regardless of how good the management or the product.

Choosing the best location

Carefully analyze the community you choose. This starts with a demographic study. Population statistics, labor force availability, per capita income, education level, and other important statistical information is available at the local library, the area college or university, and the chamber of commerce. You can find out what your particular community is spending on a product or service through the state department of revenue. These figures are valuable mainly for comparative purposes. How much is spent on your product per capita compared to national averages or the neighboring community? What is the median age? How does that relate to what you sell? If you are a manufacturer or wholesaler, what transportation means are readily available to ship your product? Refer to chapter 4 for how to use these figures to arrive at a sales projection.

It is very important to look at the competition in an area. It is possible that it is an oversaturated market. In this case, you might need to consider another town. Preferably you'll want to stay as close to your hometown as possible, because if you have been there for any time, you have made some initial contacts with bankers and potential customers. Don't underestimate the importance of potential customers from acquaintances and contacts. If your initial 12 customers are people you know, they will tell 12 people you don't know if they are pleased with your product and service. This is the start of word-of-mouth advertising. Even though it is the slowest method of becoming known, in the long run, it is the most important.

Finally, thoroughly investigate how well the businesses in the area are doing. This requires snooping around. Ask the surrounding businesses how long they have been there. A rapid turnover of space is a sign of weakness. Also, check inventory levels. Stores with empty shelves or large gaps in selection could be having credit problems. Stores overstocked with shelf-worn merchandise might be having trouble turning their stock. Many stores date their price stickers with the receiving dates of the goods. An examination of these dates can show you how quickly the merchandise turns. Another method is simply to ask the proprietors, "How's business?" You might get the runaround, but then again, you might get the truth—it can't hurt to ask.

Choosing the best site

Deciding what section of the community you want to locate in and what specific location is best for your business is the next step in choosing a location. Very simply, you let the needs of the customer decide this. Where do they expect to find your product. It might mean locating right beside your strongest competitor. The reason you find automobile dealers clustered together is that they are taking advantage of the customer traffic already generated by the competition. Keep in mind that customers are creatures of habit in their shopping patterns. Except for very unusual, specialized products or services, you must be where the customer already is. Don't overexaggerate your own importance.

If you are selling outside your business, such as a manufacturer or wholesaler does, you should be central to your main customer base. Travel costs incurred in unnecessary distance will add up. Also, extra shipping charges by being too far from your customer can hurt your financial future.

Choosing a compatible environment

Choosing an environment that matches your product or service is an important consideration. Don't place a pricey jewelry store beside a discount outlet, they don't match in market thrust. If your product only fits a certain environment, you will have no choice but to go to that environment regardless of the rent or purchase cost. Fit the location of the business to the needs of the customer. Trying to save dollars on bargain leases that don't meet the customer's accessibility requirements are foolish and will spell doom in the long run. Rent or mortgage costs are generally fixed costs. Revenues are variable. If a certain amount of sales revenues must be achieved, you must adjust other expenses around the rent costs that are necessary to achieve that revenue goal.

Understanding traffic flow

Take an actual, physical traffic count of customer exposure in the areas you are considering. For retail and service selling, you should spend time counting the walk-by and drive-by traffic. Do this at certain designated times of the day, then compare the results of potential locations to each other. The state department of transportation can assist you by providing you with automobile traffic counts for main arteries and intersections.

These studies are for comparative purposes. You will still need to compare the number of walk-by or drive-by traffic to other locations at the same time of day. This can be laborious and time consuming, but it is most important. Shopping areas can fool you if you only go by what is immediately visible. New retailers can be easily persuaded by the selling pitch of developers. For example, if the anchor store of a shopping center is a grocery store, the leasing agent will boastfully tell the potential tenant of the tremendous number of customers who shop at that store. What he fails

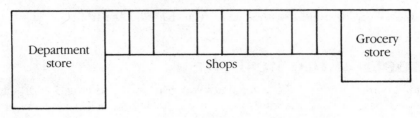

1 Anchor store center—no cross flow traffic

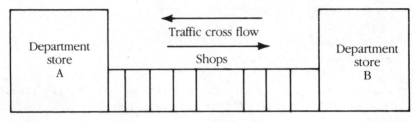

2 Anchor store center

Fig. 5–2. Layout of comparative shopping centers.

to point out is that the grocery store shopper goes in and out for a specific purpose—to buy food. They cannot put their groceries in the back seat of the car and go for a leisurely shopping tour. In addition, after paying for the groceries, they are generally not in a buying mood. Temper the agent's enthusiasm by taking a traffic count of pedestrians who are walking through the plaza. The best locations will have a cross flow of traffic between two or more major anchor stores. As the customer proceeds from one anchor store to another he or she will be forced to walk by the other tenants. Figure 5–2 illustrates two such comparative examples.

Analyzing the facilities

Closely check out the physical facilities to make sure you are getting what you think. Just as you check out a home for roof problems, plumbing inadequacies, etc., you need to check out commercial property. You might end up with the maintenance expenses, depending on your lease or purchase agreement.

At the same time, learn the history of a shopping area. Shopping areas have a life cycle. Newer shopping areas eventually replace older ones. Generally, shopping centers over 20-years-old are considered obsolete. The major stores leases might be close to expiring and they could be looking for a new area. You don't want to sign a five-year lease then watch the major stores move out, creating vacancies and leaving you with four years left on your lease.

Also, become familiar with the leasing history of the specific vacant space you are considering. Finding out the types of stores that were located in that space and why they have closed or moved could prove very enlightening. A space with a dismal history is one to avoid.

Deciding to purchase or lease

Deciding whether to purchase or lease a space is a difficult decision. Most new businesses and high-traffic retail stores will lease (see chapter 6). There are many advantages to owning a commercial location, just as there are advantages in owning a home—when the time is right. Commercial property can appreciate in value just as residential property does and can be a real plus in selling or refinancing a business. Rents are fully tax deductible, but so are interest charges on a mortgage, and there is also property depreciation allowances for an owner. There are no hard and fast rules on whether to purchase or lease a business space, because it will largely depend on the type of business you have and your long-term goals.

Pitfall #5 summary
Requirements for a good location

When choosing a location, match the site to the following list of requirements. Don't just answer "yes" or "no," defend your reasons for each answer.

1. Is the location accessible to you? Don't add to your already long hours by selecting a site that will be difficult for you to get to. If necessary, you should move to be more conveniently located to your business.

2. Is the location where your customer would expect to find such a business? Don't expect them to go out of their way to find your business. Be sure you are on the right side of the street and the right part of town.

3. Is the location in an agreeable environment for what you sell or service? Don't get caught outside the hub of activity for your type of business.

4. Is there suitable parking for customers? Also, check easements, cross easements, and right-of-way restrictions. If you're on a busy road or highway, are there acceleration lanes? Are there median cuts?

5. Is the physical facility sound and structurally safe? If remodeling extensively, be sure that current zoning and building codes will apply.

6. Is the traffic count of cars or walk-by patrons acceptable for your type of business? Don't forget the importance of being on the right side of the street. If your business is a bakery, are you on the "going-to-work" side of the road?

7. If your business requires frequent shipping or delivery, is there adequate transportation services available at reasonable costs? If you will rely very heavily on a particular supplier, is he accessible to you at a reasonable cost?

8. Is the lease or purchase agreement clearly understood? Is everything in writing?

9. Are there any sign ordinances you will have to comply with—size, place-

ment, style, etc.? Also, are there any developmental standards, such as all signs in this district must be colonial style?

10. Did you check the space measurements against the information supplied to you by the lessor or the seller to assure accuracy. The local tax assessor's office has the name and address of every property owner in the city and county *and* the legal description of the property. Including any improvements made to the property.

If you are purchasing a site for your business, you'll want to answer the following questions in addition to the previous considerations:

11. Does the comprehensive land use plan (zoning) include your type of business? Some similar business could be grandfathered in. Are you in a historical district? There could be many restrictions on use and remodeling codes.

12. At the zoning department, find out what's under construction, what's been announced to start, and what's in the process of getting approved. Is there competition on the way that you hadn't counted on? Will a road or another building be built in front of your site? Will a new anchor store or business development pull customers out of your area?

13. Are there any impact fees or local restrictions? Check with the utility and engineering departments.

14. Are there any developmental standards you might have to comply with?

15. Have you checked county and city tax structures? EPA or other federal regulatory restrictions?

Pitfall 6
Lease arrangements that can rob you

The leasing agent versus the tenant

"CHARLIE, WHY DIDN'T YOU GO OVER THIS BEFORE YOU SIGNED THE LEASE? IT CLEARLY states right here in paragraph (h) that you agree to pay six percent of sales over $146,000 as percentage rent." Laura was exasperated as she circled the paragraph and handed it to Charlie.

> (h) Percentage Rental:------6------% of gross sales in excess of $146,000.00
> ----- per month during the calendar year, payable on or before the 10th day of
> each month subject to Article IV, Section 4.3 below.

"But Laura, I had no idea what that meant. When you sent over the lease I just signed it and sent it back. You never told me about such a clause and now you want me to pay an additional $300 per month rent. It's not fair, and I can't afford it." Charlie threw the copy of the lease on Laura's desk and walked out.

"My God," thought Laura, "don't people ever read legal documents before they sign them. First-time merchants are a real pain in the neck. You have to hold their hands and explain everything word by word."

Laura couldn't help but feel sorry for Charlie. She was sure that he was totally unaware of the clause or else he would have never been selling his cigarettes at such a low price. Charlie's Tobacco Patch store was using its cigarette pricing as a loss leader to attract customers to the store, hoping that once there, they would buy enough related smoking items to offset the loss he was incurring on each carton of cigarettes. Although it did increase his sales volume, it did not increase his profits. Approximately 60 percent of his sales volume was from cigarettes that produced no gross profit. The rise in sales had pushed his volume over the point at which his lease called for percentage rent payments. Instead of not making money on the cigarettes, he was actually losing 6 percent, or six cents, on every dollar sold to the landlord. At this rate, he would soon be out of business.

Laura leaned back on her chair and closed her eyes. Being a shopping center manager and leasing agent could be contradictory. On the one hand, she was supposed to get tenants' to sign leases that were favorable to the developer, while at the same time she was to do all in her power to help them be successful. To save Charlie either the clause would have to be modified, or Charlie would have to quit selling cigarettes. She dreaded asking the developer to change the lease. She knew that a great percentage of his profits came from percentage rent. She also knew that Charlie could not stop selling cigarettes.

Understanding leasing terminology

If you don't take the time to learn the intricacies of lease arrangements, you might end up like Charlie. Charlie got caught by a clause that, had he understood at the time, he could have negotiated on different terms. As it stands, he will be extremely limited on how he operates his business.

A lease is a binding legal contract. It is similar to a bank note in that it is a financial obligation to pay each month for the duration of the contract. It does not necessarily become void if you are no longer in business. Consequently, you must look very cautiously at the terms and understand the implications over the entire term of the lease period.

Another important consideration you must keep in mind is that an agent *always* represents the seller, and it is up to you to look out for your own interests. No matter how friendly or competent your agent might seem, she is obligated by law to the seller. Unfortunately, most people are unaware that this is the case. In fact, when you buy a home today for your own personal use, you might be required to sign a paper saying that you understand this. Most agents, however, are not out to get you, just be aware of who they represent. Figure 6–1 shows the cover sheet of a lease, which is normally followed by many more pages of legal jargon. We'll use this as a reference to explain some of the different clauses.

It is important to understand that the terms of a lease are negotiable. How negotiable depends on the supply and demand for the space. Certainly, a lease in a 100 percent occupied shopping center or office complex is harder to negotiate than one in a partially occupied commercial property. The terms will also be more flexible if you are considered a desirable tenant. If you are proposing a ladies fashion store in a center that is void of ladies' fashions, you will find more favorable terms than if you are proposing to add a fourth shoe store to the tenant mix. The landlord will also be more cooperative with experienced businesses versus new businesses, because they represent more stability. He will also be more interested if you are a retail business that advertises heavily, because this adds to the overall promotion of the shopping center. Regardless of the situation, you would be foolish to accept the original landlord's proposal without testing the demand factor.

This lease, entered into this _____ day of _____, 198 _____, between the Landlord and the Tenant hereinafter named.

ARTICLE 1. Definitions and Certain Basic Provisions. 1.1

(a) "Landlord":   Smith Development Co. _____

(b) Landlord's address ___   120 Main Street
    __   Springfield, Ill. 22573 _____

(c) "Tenant": ____   Mr. John Doe DBA Gard Town _____

(d) Tenant's mailing address ___   32 Washington Ave.
    Springfield, Ill 22513 _____

(e) Tenant's trade name _____

(f) Tenant's address in Shopping Center ____   A-8

(g) "Demised Premises": approximately ____ 1200 ____ square feet in Building ____ A ____ (computed from measurements to the exterior of outside walls of the building and to the center of interior walls) having approximate dimensions of ____ 25 ____ feet x ____ 50 ____ feet such premises being shown and outlined on the plan attached hereto as Exhibit A, and being part of the Shopping Center situated upon the property described in Exhibit B attached hereto. "Shopping Center" shall refer to the property described in Exhibit B, together with such additions and other changes as Landlord may from time to time designate as included within the Shopping Center.

(h) Lease term. Commencing on the "Commencement Date" as hereinafter defined and ending ____ Thirty Six (36) ____ months thereafter except that in the event the Commencement Date is a date other than the first day of a calendar month, said term shall extend for said number of days in addition to the remainder of the calendar month following the Commencement Date.

(i) "Estimated Completion Date" day of ____ October 15, 1983 ____, 198 _____

(j) Minimum Guaranteed Rental $ ____ 729.17 * ____ per month, payable in advance.

(k) Percentage Rental ____ 6 ____ % of gross sales in excess of $ ____ 146,000.00 ____ per month during the calendar year, payable on or before the 10th day of each following month subject to Article IV, Section 4.3 below.

(l) Initial Common Area Maintenance charge per month $ ____ 52.08

(m) Initial Insurance Escrow Payment per month $ ____ 10.42

(n) Initial Tax Escrow Payment per month $ ____ 62.50

(o) "Security Deposit" $1,793.76 ____, refundable upon expiration of term less any damages for unusual wear and tear or charges necessary to restore the Demised Premises to satisfactory condition.

(p) Permitted use ____ Hallmark store — retail sale of cards and gifts

1.2 The sum of:

Minimum Guaranteed Rental as set forth in Article I, Section 1.1 (j), and	729.17*
Initial Common Area Maintenance charge, as set forth in Article I, Section 1.1 (l), and	52.08
Initial Insurance Escrow Payment as set forth in Article I, Section 1.1 (m)	10.42
Initial Tax Escrow Payment as set forth in Article I, Section 1.1 (n)	62.50
Initial Base Sales Tax Payment as set forth in Article I, Section 1.3	42.71
MONTHLY PAYMENT TOTAL	896.88

1.3 In addition to its obligation to pay the Monthly Payment Total, adjusted from time to time as provided herein, Tenant shall pay simultaneously therewith any sales tax, tax on rentals and any other charges, taxes and/or impositions now in existence or hereafter imposed by any governmental authority based upon the privilege of renting the Demised Premises or upon the amount of rent collected thereof. All payments provided for herein shall be in lawful (legal tender for public or private debt) money for the United States of America.

Fig. 6–1. Sample lease.

Understanding clauses and sub-clauses

The first point of negotiation on the lease shown in Fig. 6–1 is the term of the lease. Leases are written ranging from a month-to-month basis to 20 years. The lessor generally prefers as long as terms as possible. If this is the case, he should be willing to offer a lower rate on longer terms. Of course, you might want to have the flexibility of not committing for a long period until you have had an opportunity to experience the location. The most common duration is three to five years. What you want is the right to automatically renew the lease for an additional period of time at a designated maximum rent figure at the conclusion of the initial lease. This gives you the option. It takes away the landlord's ability to put you out in favor of another tenant, providing that you have lived up to the terms of the initial lease. The term of the renewal is generally the same as the initial term. For example, your lease might be for three years with an option to renew for an additional three years with the rent not to increase more than the cost of living index percentage since the initial term. This can be spelled out as a clause on one of the subsequent pages of the lease.

As I mentioned earlier, regardless of whether you are in business or not you are obligated to pay under the lease. Therefore, it is imperative that there be a "sublease" clause included in the body of the contract. The sublease clause allows you to transfer the lease to another party subject to landlord approval. In other words, if you are forced out of business, you or the landlord can find a replacement tenant, thereby releasing you from the obligation.

The starting date of lease payments is sometimes negotiable. It is not uncommon for a landlord to postpone payment of initial rent three to six months to give the tenant time to generate sales or as an offset for the cost of fixing up the premises. Fixing up the premises is termed leasehold improvements. Leasehold improvements are very negotiable because any attached improvements you do to the leased space become the property of the landlord. For example, carpeting, wallpaper, and built-in shelves must all be left behind when you leave. Because you are adding to the property's value, the landlord might be willing to offset these costs with rental abatements. It is definitely worth a try.

The minimum guaranteed rent is based on a cost per square foot charge. The lease in Fig. 6–1 shows 1200 square feet at a monthly charge of $729.17 per month. To get the cost per square foot, multiply the monthly rent by 12 and divide that number by the number of square feet. In this example, it conveniently works out to $7.29 per foot. The landlord might propose a base rent of $8 per square foot, you might counter with $7 and end up with $7.29.

The percentage rent clause has become very common in retail leasing. It is not to the tenant's advantage, however, because it ends up as a reward to the landlord for the tenant's hard work. The landlord believes he should be rewarded for providing such an enjoyable shopping environment. Whether you like it or not, if you are leasing in a medium to large shopping center you will probably be exposed to this type of lease. Try to work it to your advantage. It says that you will pay the minimum rent unless your sales are in excess of a breakpoint determined by the percentage factor. Of course, you'll want that percentage to be as low as possible so that it does not come into play unless your sales are far in excess of what you project. You might agree to a low percentage rent figure only if the guaranteed rent figure is lowered. Hopefully, you will have a lower base rent and a percentage figure low enough that it will never come into play or at such a point that it will be easily affordable.

There is often extra charges passed on to the tenant. Common charges include common area maintenance, real estate property taxes in excess of the base year tax on the landlord's property, dues paid to the merchant's association to be used to promote and advertise the shopping center, insurance escrow payments, and in enclosed malls, a HVAC charge to pay for the mall heating, ventilation, and air conditioning. Contemporary leases are written to assure that the landlord is covered for all operating expenses by the tenants. These extra charges are normally figured on a square foot basis and are more difficult to negotiate as they are supposedly passed on to all tenants at the same rate. Whatever they are called, they are still a form of rent and must be considered as such in figuring your operating budget for the business.

The security deposit is often arrived at by calculating the first and last month of the lease rent charges. It represents money given to the landlord—interest free—until the lease expires. Often it is negotiable to one month's total, or even none because it is an overcharged amount.

Protect yourself for future growth when agreeing to the permitted use clause. Make sure it includes wording such as "and related items." This type of vague wording makes it very difficult for the landlord to dictate what is or what isn't permitted. It is also advisable, although it is not necessarily enforceable in court, to have an exclusive clause written into the lease stating that your business will be the only one of its type in the shopping center. Many developers will bulk at this request because it represents too great of a restriction on their leasing activities. Others contend that it is legally unfair. It has been done, however, and is worth an attempt at the very least.

Finally, if you are planning to use your site right away, request that the seller have the property free of any current tenants or occupants before closing. The delay could be costly as well as frustrating.

The landlord will require that you carry property and liability insurance. The minimum amount of liability insurance coverage will be stated in the lease. This is required to protect the landlord from liability suits from any accident that might occur in your business.

It is probably a good idea to have an attorney review the lease to make sure it states what you believe it does. In case of confusion, you can add an addendum to the lease spelling out in your own terms how you believe a particular clause should be interpreted. When you consider that avoiding $200 per month on rent charges is the equivalent to $12,000 on a five-year lease, you realize the importance of favorable lease arrangements.

Pitfall #6 summary
Leasing vocabulary you should know

Before discussing a possible leasing arrangement with an agent or developer, be certain you are familiar with the following terminology:

base rent   The minimum guaranteed monthly amount that you will pay the landlord regardless of business conditions during the duration of the lease.

CAM   Acronyn for common area maintenance. Represents charges paid to the landlord for the cost of maintaining his property in suitable condition.

HVAC   Acronym for heating, ventilation, and air conditioning. Represents charges to the tenant to reimburse the landlord for the cost of utilities used in operating a commercial center.

leasehold improvements   Applies to all additions and improvements made to the landlord's property. Includes any attachments to the physical property that cannot be removed at the termination of the lease.

Merchant's Association   The organization of tenants for the purpose of jointly promoting their shopping area. Normally requires payment of monthly dues.

option to renew   The landlord has agreed that if all terms of the lease have been met satisfactory during the term of the lease, the tenant will automatically have the right to renew the lease for another term at an agreed upon rental charge.

percentage rent   The agreed upon percentage of sales that will be paid to the landlord in lieu of the base rent when that percentage total exceeds the guaranteed base rent.

Security deposit   Money held in escrow by the landlord to guarantee proper care of premises. Refundable at the termination of the lease contract.

Sublease   The tenant right to find an outside party to assume part or all liability of the lease contract. The landlord has the right of approval of the outside party.

use of premises   The stipulated purpose of the business. This is an agreed upon statement that spells out the commercial activity the tenant will be conducting.

Pitfall 7

Shortsighted financing arrangements

A manufacturer obtains a shortsighted loan

PAULA ZELSKI WAS EXCITED OVER THE PROSPECTS OF MASS PRODUCING HER OWN LINE of designer T-shirts. She had produced a limited number, 200, for distribution through three local boutiques who sold them for her on consignment. They were immediately snapped up and the phone was ringing requesting more stock and more designs.

Paula expanded her line from three designs to six and entered an agreement with Walt Crosby, a manufacturer's representative, to sell her shirts at a 15 percent commission. She built her plan around a production run of 10,000 units as follows:

Retail price	$19.95
Wholesale to retailers	9.90
Materials cost	4.00
Labor	1.50
Overhead	.80
Commission (15% of 9.90)	1.48
Net profit (before tax)	2.12

Not bad for starters, and if she could increase her production runs to 20,000, the per unit profit would increase to over $3. The initial objective was to run and sell 10,000 units followed by another run six months later giving her profits in excess of $40,000 the first year. She planned her estimate of capital needed as shown in Tables 7–1 and 7–2 to present to the bank.

Being too much in debt frightened Paula, therefore, she cut it as close as possible and requested just $15,000 over a three-year payout. The bank gave her the loan against the equity in her home.

Paula established her small production facility in a 1000 square foot space in an industrial park at a rent of $300 per month. By paying her production assistant

Table 7–1.
Start-up Costs

Fixtures & Equipment	2,150
Decorating—Remodeling	———
Installation Cost	350
Starting Inventory	12,000
Utility Deposits	250
Legal Fees & Others	400
Opening Promotion	———
Cash on Hand	1,800
Other	
Total paid only once exp.	16,950

Table 7–2.
Start-up Business Plan

Item	Estimated Monthly Expense Col I	Months X	= Col II
Owner's Salary		3	
Other Salary	1,000	3	3,000
*Rent	300	3	900
Advertising	50	3	150
Supplies	100	3	300
Telephone-Utilities	220	3	660
Accounting		3	
Insurance	65	3	195
Loan Principal and Interest	140	3	420
Taxes	—	3	
Miscellaneous		3	
Total month expense	1,875		

$1,000 per month, she was able to keep within her $1,800 per month projected operating budget.

Once all of the equipment was installed and the first production run was paid for, she had just barely over $1,800—one month's operating expenses—left in her checking account. Otherwise, everything looked great. Walt had easily sold the entire 10,000 units at the regional fashion show in Atlanta.

Paula worked like crazy for the next three months to get the orders filled, but still had trouble meeting some of the ship dates. She ran into cash flow problems because she had done a very poor job of planning for accounts receivable. Her operating account ran out before shipments were made. Although roughly half of the accounts were C.O.D., it still took turnaround time to receive any income. Merchandise sold on terms would average 60 days before collection. There was no money to meet payroll, rent, or additional materials. In addition, Walt was upset as he had expected to receive some of his commission on sale, not on account payment. Paula was forced to borrow short-term money to hold her over at an interest rate 4 percent higher than her long-term note.

Eventually, she collected and paid all concerned, including the short-term note. The additional interest charges reduced her net profit percentage and two accounts returned shipments due to late arrival. Although the profit was slim, the product reception was tremendous. Walt came back from the next show with orders for 18,000 units.

Paula's elation quickly turned to panic as she realized that to run a production run this size would require close to $70,000 in materials, not to mention labor. Her income from the first run, after expenses, would not come close. The only answer seemed to borrow again on a short-term basis at the higher interest rate. Even if she got the loan, the higher interest rate would really dig into her profits. She wished she had done a better job of arranging the initial long-term financing.

Understanding cash flow

In her excitement of getting her business started, Paula did what many new entrepreneurs do, she didn't look at the full picture. She will survive this, but it will be expensive and frustrating. Bankers do not react well to changes in plans. When a loan committee approves a loan, they look to the officer who made the recommendation for responsibility. These officers do not like to go back three months later and explain why a new account needs more money. It should have been foreseen at the initial proposal. Between the customer's reluctance to request more long-term assistance and the officer's reluctance to make the additional request to the committee, it is easier to put together short-term arrangements to hold the customer over. Unfortunately, these are more expensive and more difficult to handle as far as the payment terms. Proper planning of your financial needs allows you to have a more convenient payout program at a lower interest rate.

Proper financing requires more than just getting the doors open, however. Arrangements must be made to allow the business to operate at top efficiency, not hampered by cash flow problems. The aspiring entrepreneur will normally put together a pro forma (projected) income statement and balance sheet. These necessary tools show the anticipated condition of the business at certain intervals (annual, semiannual, quarterly), but fail to take into consideration the daily operating conditions of the business. This requires cash flow planning.

Cash flow shows the money in and out of a business, not profit. There is a difference. A seasonal business that does well at Christmas will show a nice profit on its income statement at the end of the Christmas quarter, however, it will not show how the business survived October and November to get to December 25. A cash flow statement shows cash receipts as opposed to sales and what will actually be paid at a certain time as opposed to what was invoiced. A sample cash flow statement is shown in Fig. 7–1.

Trouble spots will show up on the cash available line at the end of some months. To sell $10,000 in a month does not mean you receive $10,000 in the month. Any

MONTHLY CASH

See Reverse Side for Instructions and Public Comment Information

NAME OF BUSINESS		ADDRESS			OWNER		

	Pre-Start-up Position		1		2		3		4		5	
YEAR MONTH	Estimate	Actual	Estimate	Actual	Estimate	Actual	Estimate	Actual	Estimate	Actual	Estimate	Actual
1. CASH ON HAND (Beginning of month)												
2. CASH RECEIPTS												
(a) Cash Sales												
(b) Collections from Credit Accounts												
(c) Loan or Other Cash injection (Specify)												
3. TOTAL CASH RECEIPTS (2a + 2b + 2c = 3)												
4. TOTAL CASH AVAILABLE (Before cash out) (1 + 3)												
5. CASH PAID OUT												
(a) Purchases (Merchandise)												
(b) Gross Wages (Excludes withdrawals)												
(c) Payroll Expenses (Taxes, etc.)												
(d) Outside Services												
(e) Supplies (Office and operating)												
(f) Repairs and Maintenance												
(g) Advertising												
(h) Car, Delivery, and Travel												
(i) Accounting and Legal												
(j) Rent												
(k) Telephone												
(l) Utilities												
(m) Insurance												
(n) Taxes (Real estate, etc.)												
(o) Interest												
(p) Other Expenses (Specify each)												
(q) Miscellaneous (Unspecified)												
(r) Subtotal												
(s) Loan Principal Payment												
(t) Capital Purchases (Specify)												
(u) Other Start-up Costs												
(v) Reserve and/or Escrow (Specify)												
(w) Owner's Withdrawal												
6. TOTAL CASH PAID OUT (Total 5a thru 5w)												
7. CASH POSITION (End of month) (4 minus 6)												
ESSENTIAL OPERATING DATA (Non-cash flow information) A. Sales Volume (Dollars)												
B. Accounts Receivable (End of month)												
C. Bad Debt (End of month)												
D. Inventory on Hand (End of month)												
E. Accounts Payable (End of month)												
F. Depreciation												

SBA FORM 1100 (1-83) REF: SOP 60 10 Previous Editions Are Obsolete

Fig. 7-1. Cash flow worksheet.

FLOW PROJECTION

Form Approval:
OMB No 3245-0019
Expires: 8-31-91

| TYPE OF BUSINESS | | | | PREPARED BY | | | | DATE | | |

6		7		8		9		10		11		12		TOTAL		
														Columns 1—12		
Estimate	Actual	Estimate	Actual	Estimate	Actual	Estimate	Actual	Estimate	Actual	Estimate	Actual	Estimate	Actual	Estimate	Actual	
																1.
																2.
																(a)
																(b)
																(c)
																3.
																4.
																5.
																(a)
																(b)
																(c)
																(d)
																(e)
																(f)
																(g)
																(h)
																(i)
																(j)
																(k)
																(l)
																(m)
																(n)
																(o)
																(p)
																(q)
																(r)
																(s)
																(t)
																(u)
																(v)
																(w)
																6.
																7.
																A.
																B.
																C.
																D.
																E.
																F.

business that is not strictly cash sales, must take into account account receivables. A reserve fund must be created that covers outstanding money. If the average collection time is 37 days, 10 percent of all receipts (37 days/365 days) will always be outstanding until the business liquidates or is sold. Therefore, if the business has a projected sales of $250,000, $25,000 must be set aside from the beginning. A good financing plan projects this and reserves this money for future needs.

One of your objectives is to build a sound relationship with your lending institution. More than likely, there will be expansions and additions in the future that will require their assistance. A good plan now will show them your dependability and reliability. Take your time in your considerations of what your financing needs are now and what they will be in the future.

Finding the best source of money

Now that you have put together your five-year proforma, a balance sheet, and made cash flow projections, you need to find the best source for financial assistance. If you are just starting out, you are headed for a rude awakening if you think the banks are anxiously awaiting your arrival. Building a sound relationship with a bank takes time. Bankers and aspiring entrepreneurs do not make a good match. You are a risk taker, they are not. They want complete assurance of being paid back, particularly for a new business, which means they want assured collateral. The collateral must be easily liquidated, such as stocks, bonds, CD's, homes, or automobiles. Inventory, accounts receivables, and personal belongings are not considered liquidable. If you do not have the necessary collateral, banks are not the answer for seed money. It will have to come from you, your friends, trade credit, relatives, or investors.

Most initial financing is an assortment of contributors, although you will have to put up enough of your own money to show confidence in your plan. Your confidence and enthusiasm might also generate interest from outside parties or relatives. A certain amount of assistance might be available within the industry, particularly in regards to equipment purchases made on installment plans, with the equipment being held as collateral. Once your plan is 90 percent in order, you can visit the bank for short-term operating capital. This is important, because once you establish a credit relationship with a bank and perform well, they will be much more receptive in the future.

Outside sources include investors, joint venture capitalists, and partners. All of which require giving up a combination of power and profits. Usually, you would only seek this type of help if you were absolutely confident of large profits or needed assistance in the form of technical help. There is a misconception that the government has grant programs available for small businesses. Grants mean free money and this does not exist with the exception of some nonprofit firms working in disadvantaged sectors of the economy.

The other possible borrowing source is the Small Business Administration (SBA) guaranteed loan program. This program is similar to a bank loan. In fact, the money does come from a bank, which is guaranteed by the government that, if something happens to the business, the government will pay up to 90 percent of the loan amount. In order to qualify, a borrower must first have been turned down by at least two commercial banks. The reason for this is that the government will not interfere with the private sector of banking unless it is a last resort. SBA loans still require collateral, however, the terms are more flexible and more consideration is given to the potential of the business plan. Generally, the range of these loans are $50,000 to $750,000 at an interest rate based on a fully secured loan.

For financial assistance guidance, look to the industry you will be becoming a part of for suggestions, find a banker who is willing to get involved, visit government advisors such as the SBA, Small Business Development Centers, or SCORE offices. Also, there are private financial advisors such as accountants and small business consultants. The main consideration is that whoever you use be knowledgeable, or willing to become knowledgeable, of the industry you are pursuing.

Pitfall #7 summary
SBA loan guarantees

The following is a description of terms for SBA loans, which are available as direct loans or guaranteed bank loans. Most SBA loans are in the form of guarantees to the lending bank that the government will stand behind the borrower in case of default. Borrowers have to be turned down by only one bank to be eligible to apply for a Guaranteed loan through a bank. A decline letter is not required. The "Lender's Application for Guaranty or Participation, SBA Form 4–I, covers that. Two bank decline letters are required for a Direct loan if the population is 200,000 or more, one letter if the population is under 200,000.

Guaranteed loans

Maximum SBA exposure is $750,000. Approximately 30 percent equity injection is required (approximately 25 percent for all veterans). Full collateral for the borrowed amount is required (the business itself, plus real estate, or other personal assets).

Interest rates

The interest rates for loans are:

- Maximum, $2^3/_4$ percent above prime for loans of seven years or more.
- Maximum, $2^1/_4$ percent above prime for loans under seven years.
- Banks almost always choose to go with a floating rate, adjusted quarterly.

Prepayment terms

The following are the maximum repayment terms for all loans:

7 years	Operating capital only
10 years	Combination of everything, except real estate
25 years	Real estate position only. Terms for combinations, including real estate, vary according to percentage of proceeds used for non-real estate purposes.

There is a guaranty fee of 2 percent of the guaranteed amount that is passed along to the borrower. This fee is paid to the SBA. Keep in mind that Metro Atlanta banks will not participate in SBA loans of less than $50,000. (That is the borrowed amount, after 25 to 30 percent equity injection.) The C&S Bank, and possibly others, will not consider SBA loans of less than $100,000.

Direct loans

The terms of a direct loan are as follows:

- The maximum direct loan is $150,000.
- The interest rate is fixed for the term of the loan. The rate for new loans is announced quarterly.
- Direct loan funding is extremely limited, and all loans are funded on a case-by-case basis.

There are three Direct loan programs:

1. Vietnam-era and Disabled Veterans
2. Handicapped Assistance (HAL I, sheltered workshops and HAL II, individuals)
3. 7(a)ll Loans (high unemployment areas and low-income individuals)

Keep in mind that all Direct loan applications must essentially meet the same requirements as those for banks.

Vietnam-era and disabled veterans loan program

The following outlines the terms of the Direct loan programs for Vietnam-era and disabled veterans:

1. Vietnam-era veterans are those veterans who served on active duty for more than 180 days, any part of which was between August 5, 1964 and May 7, 1975. Disabled veterans are Vietnam-era veterans discharged for service-connected disability, veterans with 30 percent or more compensable disability, or veterans with a disability discharge.
2. Veterans must have been discharged other than dishonorably.
3. Fifty-one percent veteran ownership is required and the veteran must participate in the actual day-to-day operations of the business.
4. There is a $150,000 maximum loan amount.
5. It is a one-time opportunity.
6. A fixed interest rate is offered for the term of the loan.
7. The maximum terms are seven years (operating capital only), 10 years (combination, except real estate), 25 years (real estate position only. Combinations vary with use of proceeds).
8. The requirements are the same as for bank loans: 25 percent equity injection in the business, reasonable assurance of ability to repay the loan from business earnings, and adequate collateral.

9. Applicant must demonstrate that funds are not otherwise available on reasonable terms and provide evidence that the loan was rejected other than for credit reasons and on the same or similar terms that are sought from the SBA. Two letters of decline are required from two separate lending institutions if the population is 200,000 or more, one letter if the population is under 200,000. By law, the agency cannot make a direct loan if funds can be obtained from a private source.

10. Loans for the following purposes are not eligible:
    ~nonprofit organizations
    ~publishing, broadcast media, or any other firms dealing with the creation, origination, expression, or distribution of ideas, values, thoughts, or opinions
    ~floor planning for new or used cars
    ~gambling
    ~speculation
    ~real property held primarily for sale or investment
    ~lending or investment
    ~pyramid sales plans
    ~illegal activities
    ~persons on parole or probation or persons who have criminal cases pending against them
    ~debt consolidation

Finally, when applying for a Direct Vietnam-Era or Disabled Veteran's loan, you must attach the following documents to the SBA loan application:

1. Copy of Form DD 214

2. Two decline letters (see item #9)

3. Veterans Administration documentation for disabled veterans

Pitfall 8

Choosing the wrong organizational structure

The business owner who paid taxes on his losses

"THE GOOD NEWS, BEN, IS THAT THE CORPORATION DOESN'T OWE ANY TAXES THIS year. The bad news is that it lost $20,000." Gloria handed Ben the tax return for his review.

"What about my personal tax return Gloria? I must be getting back some money."

"I am afraid not, Ben. Since you formed a corporation, the salary paid to you as president must be declared as fully taxable income, regardless of how the corporation did. If you had been a proprietorship, partnership, or a subchapter S corporation, you could have deducted the $20,000 as a business loss, but not as an employee of a corporation."

"But Gloria, it was still my loss, the same as when I was a proprietorship. It doesn't seem fair."

Ben had switched to a corporation believing that his profits would be better protected from taxes. Gloria, his accountant, had concurred with the idea. In his enthusiasm of building a successful business, he had not considered that he might lose money. All he cared about was that, as a corporation, he could deduct his insurance, have better protection against personal liability suits, and a lower tax rate against profits.

The years that followed further illustrated Ben's poor decision. He continued to pay taxes on the full amount of his annual salary of $30,000, even though the corporation seldom showed a profit. In five years, he calculated that he had paid an additional $25,000 to the IRS in personal taxes that could have been avoided if he had decided on a different form of organization.

Sole proprietorships, partnerships, and corporations

Your choice of whether your business should be a proprietorship, a partnership, or a corporation can be important for many reasons. Each has advantages and disadvantages depending on the type of activity you are engaged in.

Being a proprietor is the simplest. It is often the suggested way for a new business that does not carry great personal liability threats. When you are a proprietorship you are simply "doing business as" the name of your business. You are personally responsible for all activity of the business. As such, you declare all profits or losses in any calendar year as yours. If you make a $20,000 profit, you show it on your 1040 personal tax form and pay the taxes on that figure. Likewise, if you lose $20,000, you can deduct that amount from your gross income. Realistically, most new businesses do not (initially) show profits, and it might be the way to start. You will be able to change your status to a corporation, if advisable, at a later date. There are certain deductions, particularly in the formidable years, that can be used to your personal advantage, such as depreciation.

Depreciation is the deductible expense for the wear and use of capital equipment. Whether it is machinery, fixtures, cash registers, or leasehold improvements, any equipment used to conduct business represents possible depreciable items. The IRS allows you to, at least on paper, show a certain amount of revenue as put aside to replace this equipment as it wears out. There are various depreciation schedules you can use to write this expense off. The most common is seven years. For example, if your capital investment for equipment, machinery or fixtures is $50,000, you will be able to deduct $7,000 to $10,000 per year as a fully deductible expense on your tax income statement. For many, this deduction can be used as money to be paid from until the business is more stable.

A proprietorship is simple to form. It requires no formal agreements because there are no other parties involved. The owner simply needs to secure the necessary licenses, tax identification numbers, and certifications in his or her own name, and you will be in business.

A partnership, however, is generally the least advisable way to go. It involves two or more individuals coming together to engage in a business activity. The tax structure is the same as a proprietorship except the profits and losses of the partnership are divided by an agreed upon percentage by the partners. Because a partnership involves more than one person, it requires writing a partnership agreement to spell out the specifics of the agreement. Although this agreement is not a legal requirement, anyone who enters a partnership without writing out these guidelines is asking for trouble. Things have a way of changing and people forgetting over time, so it is essential that there be a signed document that all abide by. Figure 8–1 shows a sample partnership agreement.

A partnership requires filing a separate partnership tax return, does not carry liability protection for general partners, and can lead into legal and personal disputes. A corporate form of ownership is generally recognized as preferable over a partnership, because it can serve the same purpose while offering a cleaner and better protected structure for the owners.

SAMPLE PARTNERSHIP AGREEMENT

Agreement made on _____, 19__, between _____ of _____, City of _____ County of _____, State of _____, and _____ of _____(address), City of _____, County of _____, State of _____, hereinafter referred to as partners.

ITEM ONE: NAME, PURPOSE, AND DOMICILE

The name of the partnership shall be _____. The partnership shall be conducted for the purposes of _____. The principal place of business shall be at _____ _____ unless relocated by majority consent of the partners.

ITEM TWO: DURATION OF AGREEMENT

The term of this agreement shall be for _____ years, commencing on _____, 19__. and terminating on _____, 19__, unless sooner terminated by mutual consent of the parties or by operation of the provisions of this agreement.

ITEM THREE: CONTRIBUTION

Each partner shall contribute _____ Dollars ($_____) on or before _____, 19__ to be used by the partnership to establish its capital position. Any additional contribution required of partners shall only be determined and established in accordance with Items Seven and Seventeen.

ITEM FOUR: BOOKS AND RECORDS

Books of accounts shall be maintained by the partners, and proper entries made therein of all sales, purchases, receipts, payments, transactions, and property of the partnership, and the books of accounts and all records of the partnership shall be retained at the principal place of business as specified in Item One herein. Each partner shall have free access at all times to all books and records maintained relative to the partnership business.

ITEM FIVE: DIVISION OF PROFITS AND LOSSES

Each partner shall be entitled to _____ percent (_____%) of the net profits of the business and all losses occuring in the course of the business shall be borne in the same proportion, unless the losses are occasioned by the wilful neglect or default, and not mere mistake or error, of any of the partners, in which case the loss so incurred shall be made good by the partner through whose neglect or default the losses shall arise. Distribution of profits shall be made on the _____ day of _____ each year.

ITEM SIX: PERFORMANCE

Each partner shall apply all of his experience, training, and ability in discharging his assigned functions in the partnership and in the performance of all work that may be necessary or advantageous to further business interests of the partnership.

ITEM SEVEN: BUSINESS EXPENSES

The rent of the buildings where the partnership business shall be carried on, and the cost of repairs and alterations, all rates, taxes, payments for insurance, and other expenses in respect to the buildings used by the partnership, and the wages for all persons employed by the partnership are all to become payable on the account of the partnership. All losses incurred shall be paid out of the capital of the partnership or the profits arising from the partnership business, or, if both shall be deficient, by the partners on a pro rata basis, in proportion to their original contributions.

ITEM EIGHT: ACCOUNTING

The fiscal year of the partnership shall be from _____ to _____ of each year. On the _____ day of

Fig. 8–1. Sample partnership agreement.

_____ commencing in 19___, and on the _____ day of _____ in each succeeding year, a general accounting shall be made and taken by the partners of all sales, purchases, receipts, payments, and transactions of the partnership during the preceding fiscal year, and all the capital property and current liabilities of the partnership. The general accounting shall be written in the partnership account books and signed in each book by each partner immediately after it is completed. After the signature of each partner is entered, each partner shall keep one set (copy) of records and shall be bound by every account, except that if any manifest error is found therein by any partner and shown to the

other partners within _____ months after the error shall have been noted by all of them, the error shall be rectified.

ITEM NINE: SEPARATE DEBTS

No partner shall enter into any bond or become surety, security, bail or co-signer for any person, partnership or corporation, or knowingly condone anything whereby the partnership property may be attached or be taken in execution, without the written consent of the other partners.

Each partner shall punctually pay his separate debts and indemnity the other partners and the capital and property of the partnership against his separate debts and all expenses relating thereto.

ITEM TEN: AUTHORITY

No partner shall buy any goods or articles or enter into any contract exceeding the value of _____ Dollars ($_____) without the prior consent in writing of the other partners: or the other partners shall have the option to take the goods or accept the contract on account of the partnership or let the goods remain the sole property of the partner who shall have obligated himself.

ITEM ELEVEN: EMPLOYEE MANAGEMENT

No partner shall hire or dismiss any person in the employment of the partnership without the consent of the other partners, except in case of gross misconduct by the employee.

ITEM TWELVE: SALARY

No partner shall receive any salary from the partnership, and the only compensation to be paid shall be as provided in Items Five and Fourteen herein.

ITEM THIRTEEN: DEATH OF PARTNER

In the event of the death of one partner, the legal representative of the deceased partner shall remain as a partner in the firm, except that the exercising of the right on the part of the representative of the deceased partner shall not

continue for a period in excess of _____ months, even though under the terms hereof a greater period of time is provided before the termination of this agreement. The original rights of the partners herein shall accrue to their heirs, executors, or assigns.

ITEM FOURTEEN: ADVANCE DRAWS

Each partner shall be at liberty to draw out of the business in anticipation of the expected profits any sums that may be mutually agreed on, and the sums are to be drawn only after there has been entered in the books of the partnership the terms of agreement, giving the date, the amount to be drawn by the respective partners, the time at which the sums shall be drawn, and any other conditions or matters mutually agreed on. The signatures of each partner shall be affixed thereon. The total sum of the advance draw for each partner shall be deducted from the sum that partner is entitled to under the distribution of profits as provided for in Item Five of this agreement.

ITEM FIFTEEN: RETIREMENT

In the event any partner shall desire to retire from the partnership, he shall give ____ months notice in writing to

the other partners and the continuing partners shall pay to the retiring partner at the termination of the ____ months notice the value of the interest of the retiring partner in the partnership. The value shall be determined by a closing of the books and a rendition of the appropriate profit and loss, trial balance, and balance sheet statements. All disputes arising therefrom shall be determined as provided in Item Eighteen.

ITEM SIXTEEN: RIGHTS OF CONTINUING PARTNERS

On the retirement of any partner, the continuing partners shall be at liberty, if they so desire, to retain all trade names designating the firm name used, and each of the partners shall sign and execute assignments, instruments, or papers that shall be reasonably required for effectuating an amicable retirement.

ITEM SEVENTEEN: ADDITIONAL CONTRIBUTIONS

The partners shall not have to contribute any additional capital to the partnership to that required under Item Three herein, except as follows: (1) each partner shall be required to contribute a proportionate share in additional contributions if the fiscal year closes with an insufficiency in the capital account or profits of the partnership to meet current expenses, or (2) the capital account falls below _____ Dollars ($_____) for a period of _____ months.

ITEM EIGHTEEN: ARBITRATION

If any differences shall arise between or among partners as to their rights or liabilities under this agreement, or under any instrument made in furtherance of the partnership business, the difference shall be determined and the instrument shall be settled by _____, acting as arbitrator, and his decision shall be final as to the contents and interpretations of the instrument and as to the proper mode of carrying the provision into effect.

ITEM NINETEEN: RELEASE OF DEBTS

No partner shall compound, release, or discharge any debt that shall be due or owing to the partnership, without receiving the full amount thereof, unless that partner obtains the prior written consent of the other partners to the discharge of the indebtedness.

ITEM TWENTY: ADDITIONS, ALTERATIONS, OR MODIFICATIONS

Where it shall appear to the partners that this agreement, or any terms and condition contained herein, are in any way ineffective or deficient, or not expressed as originally intended, and any alterations or addition shall be deemed necessary, the partners will enter into, execute and perform all further deeds and instruments as their counsel shall advise. Any addition, alteration, or modification shall be in writing, and no oral agreement shall be effective.

In witness whereof, the parties have executed this agreement on _____, the day and year first above written.

Fig. 8-1. Continued.

Forming a corporation

When you form a corporation, you actually create a new entity in the world that is born to conduct business. It has all the legal rights of an individual in regards to conducting commercial activity. It can sue, be sued, own property, sell property, and sell the rights of ownership in the form of exchanging stock for money. As such, it is responsible for the activities it engages in, not necessarily the stockholders. If you are the president and principal owner of a corporation, you are an employee of that corporation. In the event there is a suit brought against the company, it will be brought against the corporation, not against you personally. The assets of the corporation would be in jeopardy, not your personal assets. As a proprietorship or partnership, the owners can be sued personally for the activity of the business. This is a very important consideration if you are engaged in an industry that has a high occurrence of liability suits. This is what is called *limited liability*. If your business is at risk, you have no choice but to incorporate immediately. You should discuss this with an attorney, however, before deciding. He or she will be able to point out in what areas this limited liability features applies and what areas you might still be personally responsible for. As a small corporation owner, you will often be requested to sign personally in agreements such as bank notes or leases. This will nullify the corporation protection. Understand the pros and cons of this protection before proceeding.

There are other advantages to the corporation. As an employee, the corporation can pay your insurance as a deductible expense, possibly buy a business automobile for your use, and create a pension plan for your retirement. These and other employee benefits are deductible to the corporation and will reduce your tax exposure. Although the taxes on corporate profits have pretty much evened out with personal tax rates, there are generally more avenues available to protect profits as a corporation. In a highly profitable mature business, a corporation is the preferred form of organizational structure.

For small, tightly controlled corporations, a subchapter S corporation is the most popular method of incorporation. It provides the best of both worlds. The owners are able to treat their tax reporting on the same basis as a proprietorship or partnership while at the same time receiving the benefit of limited liability. It has restrictions as to the number of stockholders allowed and how stock can be bought and sold, but generally, they don't handicap the small or family-held business. Take the time to review this option. It could be a viable alternative to a sole proprietorship or partnership.

A corporation can easily substitute for a partnership. The only legitimate reasons for inviting outside associates into your business is for either raising money or adding technical expertise. The corporation allows you to raise money by selling stock, which can be sold in whatever percentage you want. An equal partnership can be created by selling 50 percent of the stock to another party. Instead of a partnership agreement, you write out bylaws of the corporation. Appendix B contains corporate bylaws.

Pitfall #8 summary
Sample incorporation procedure

The following is an example of a corporation filing procedure. Check with your state for its own specific procedure. It is not difficult to file for a corporation. By doing it yourself, you will save considerable legal expense.

FILING PROCEDURES FOR INCORPORATING
A GEORGIA PROFIT OR NONPROFIT CORPORATION
Effective: July 1, 1989

These instructions explain the procedure for filing Articles of Incorporation for a Georgia corporation (profit or nonprofit) pursuant to O.C.G.A. §14-2-101 et seq. ("Code"). The matters set forth herein apply to the filing requirements of the Code and are not intended to provide legal, tax or business advice concerning business corporations. You are encouraged to seek private counsel prior to incorporation.

The Secretary of State's Office is the granting authority for all corporations created under the laws of this state and is the filing depository for related papers and reports required under the Code. A business obtains corporate authority in Georgia by the following procedure:

A. NAME RESERVATION. The proposed name for the corporation may be reserved with the Secretary of State for a non-renewable 60-day period. The incorporator or the attorney may request that the Secretary of State search the files of existing Georgia corporations, qualified foreign corporations and limited partnerships. If the name is distinguishable from other business names and thereby available, a verification number is issued. This procedure may be accomplished by sending to the Secretary of State the attached form, "Application for Reservation of a Name", or by calling **(404) 656-2817.** Articles of Incorporation may be submitted without a prior name reservation, but if the desired name is not distinguishable, the articles will be returned. **Filing fees are nonrefundable. However, in the case of a deficient filing, the fees may be applied to the corrected documents.**

B. ARTICLES OF INCORPORATION. The incorporator or attorney for the corporation must prepare the Articles of Incorporation in the proper format as prescribed by O.C.G.A. §14-2-202 (profit) or O.C.G.A. §14-3-131 (nonprofit). The Articles of Incorporation must be presented for filing in accordance with O.C.G.A. §14-2-202. The attached sample format of Articles of Incorporation may be used as a guide to assist in the preparation of the articles. Type the Articles of Incorporation using the sample only as a guide. Please do not use the sample as a form.

C. PUBLISHER'S LETTER AND FEE. The applicant's signature on Form A100 certifies that a publication letter has been forwarded to the appropriate newspaper, along with the fee, as mandated by O.C.G.A. §14-2-201.1. The publisher's letter and fees are no longer required to be filed with the Secretary of State. Failure to publish as required by the Code may result in the administrative dissolution of the corporation.

NOTE: Filing corporate documents with the county office of the Clerk of Superior Court is no longer required.

D. ORDER OF DOCUMENTS. The following documents must be presented to the Secretary of State:

1. **FORM A100.** (Data Entry Form) This form is the transmittal document. The filing fee must be submitted by a check in the amount of $60.00 made payable to the Secretary of State. This form sould be carefully completed since information from it is used in maintaining the Secretary of State corporate database. Completion instructions are on the back of this form.

2. **ORIGINAL ARTICLES.** The original Articles

of Incorporation must be manually signed by the chairman of the board of directors, the president or another corporate officer. If these positions have not been selected, an incorporator may sign. The signer must denote in what capacity he is signing the document. Information requested on form A100 must be included in the articles. See the attached sample format for other items to be included. There are many other business, financial and tax statements that may be included in the articles. The incorporator should seek private counsel to determine what elective information should be included.

3.   **NAME VERIFICATION.** If a name is reserved prior to filing the Articles of Incorporation, the name reservation certificate or a verification number should be attached. Failure to verify or reserve the name may result in the name not being available and the return of your filing.

E.   **SECRETARY OF STATE EXAMINATION.** The Secretary of State provides only a ministerial review of the incorporation documents to determine if they comply with the minimum filing requirements of the Code. The Secretary will not review for matters such as tax status, corporate finance or compliance with other business or regulatory laws. If the documents are acceptable, an original certificate or stamp of incorporation will be attached to a copy and returned to the incorporator or the filing attorney. The certificate will reflect the date on which documents were received by the Secretary of State. If the documents are incorrect and not acceptable for filing, they will be returned with a deficiency notice.

F.   **NONPROFIT ORGANIZATIONS.** The following stipulations may or may not apply to the registration of a nonprofit organization.

1.   **NONPROFIT TAX STATUS.** Private counsel should be consulted to determine the exact wording for the Articles of Incorporation for a nonprofit corporation. Failure to have appropriate wording may seriously affect the corporation's tax status. Once incorporated, the only way to change the articles is to file amended articles and pay all fees required for such a filing. Corporations organized under the nonprofit statutes of the various states in the U.S. do not automatically qualify for exemption from federal income tax. You should contact the Internal Revenue Service to apply for

tax-exempt status. Tax forms and publications can be obtained by telephoning the IRS's "forms only" number, 1-800-424-FORM.

2. **CHARITABLE ORGANIZATIONS.** If a nonprofit organization will be soliciting or accepting charitable contributions in Georgia, it must file a charitable registration with the Secretary of State O.C.G.A. §43-17-5. This registration is in addition to and separate from a corporate

filing. Information regarding charitable registration can be obtained by contacting this office at (404) 656-4910.

The Secretary of State encourages corporate formation in Georgia. The Business Services and Regulation staff will assist in any way possible to the filing of corporate documents.

MAX CLELAND
SECRETARY OF STATE

BY: *James F. Gullion*

JAMES F. GULLION, Director
Business Services and Regulation

Form A-99, Revised 5/89

Attachments: A100 Form
Application for Reservation of a Name
Sample Format-Articles of Incorporation
Sample Format-Notice of Intent to Incorporate

BUSINESS SERVICES AND REGULATION
Suite 315, West Tower
2 Martin Luther King Jr. Drive
Atlanta, Georgia 30334
404-656-2817 (Information)

MAX CLELAND
Secretary of State
State of Georgia

J. F. GULLION
Director

Form A 300	APPLICATION FOR RESERVATION OF A NAME	Eff. 7/89

Your Name and Address in this Block

Signature: Date: Telephone Number:

Pursuant to O.C.G.A. Section 14-2-401, the above applies to reserve the following corporate name for a nonrenewable 60-day period. Georgia law requires that the corporate name shall contain the word "corporation," "company", "incorporated," "limited," or an abbreviation of one of such words. The name shall not in any instance exceed 80 characters, including spaces and punctuation.

LIST NAME CHOICES IN ORDER OF PREFERENCE:

1. _____
2. _____
3. _____

☐ For Domestic Use (Georgia Corporation)   ☐ Profit

☐ For Foreign Use (Out-of-State Corporation)   ☐ Non-Profit

☐ Mail   Federal Express: Other:

Completed by: Date: Telephone Number:

☐ See reverse for explanation if this request has been returned.

NAME RESERVATION REQUEST

RETURN FORM

The records of this office indicate that the name marked on the front of this form:

☐ Is not available for use as a corporation in Georgia because it is identical to or not distinguishable from another corporation of record.

☐ Is available only with a letter of consent from the following corporation:

MAX CLELAND
Secretary of State
State of Georgia

BUSINESS SERVICES AND REGULATION
Suite 315, West Tower
2 Martin Luther King Jr., Drive
Atlanta, Georgia 30334
(404) 656-2817

A100

Eff. 7/1/89
J. F. GULLION
Director

ARTICLES OF INCORPORATION DATA ENTRY FORM
FOR GEORGIA CORPORATIONS

I.   Filing Date: _____ Code:_____ Docket Number: _____

Assigned Exam: _____ Amount: $ _____ By: _____

Charter Number: _____ Completed: _____

DO NOT WRITE ABOVE THIS LINE – SOS USE ONLY

NOTICE TO APPLICANT: PRINT PLAINLY OR TYPE THE REMAINDER OF THIS FORM.

II.   Corporate Name:

Mailing Address:

City: County: State: Zip Code:

III. Fees Submitted By:

Amount Enclosed: $ Check Number:

IV.   Incorporator:

Address:

City: State: Zip Code:

Incorporator:

Address:

City: State: Zip Code:

V.   Registered Agent/Office:

Address:

City: County: State: Zip Code:

VI. ARTICLES OF INCORPORATION FILING CHECK-OFF LIST	Applicant	Examiner
1. Original and one conformed copy of Articles of Incorporation		
2. Corporate name verification number		
3. Authorized shares stated		
4. Incorporator's signature		
5. Post effective date, if applicable		
6. Number of pages attached:		

VII. Applicant/Attorney: Telephone:

Address:

City: State: Zip Code:

**NOTICE: Attach original and one copy of the Articles of Incorporation and the Secretary of State filing fee ($60.00).
Mail or deliver to the above address. This form does not replace the Articles of Incorporation.**

**I understand that the information on this form will be used in the Secretary of State Corporate database. I certify that a
notice of Intent to Incorporate and a publishing fee of $40.00 has been mailed or delivered to an authorized newspaper,
as required by law.**

Signed:_____   Date: _____

Eff. 7/1/89

INSTRUCTIONS FOR COMPLETING FORM A100

THIS FORM MUST BE FILED WITH ALL NEW GEORGIA CORPORATIONS. The form must be typed or plainly printed. This will allow the information to be entered in the Secretary of State corporate information database. THIS FORM DOES NOT REPLACE THE ARTICLES OF INCORPORATION.

I.   SECRETARY OF STATE USE ONLY. Do not write in this section. It is reserved for Secretary of State use only.

II.   CORPORATE NAME AND MAILING ADDRESS. List the exact corporate name and mailing address for the proposed corporation's initial corporate office. O.C.G.A. 14-2-202(a)(5)

III. FEES. List information concerning the payment of Secretary of State filing fees ($60.00). O.C.G.A. 14-2-122 Checks should be made payable to the Secretary of State. NOTE: Signature at bottom of form certifies that notice of Intent to Incorporate with the publishing fee has been delivered to the appropriate publisher. O.C.G.A. 14-2-201.1

IV.   INCORPORATOR. List the name and address of each incorporator. O.C.G.A. 14-2-202(a)(4) If space does not allow, attachment will be accepted.

V.   REGISTERED AGENT. List the name of the registered agent. List the exact business address and county in Georgia of the registered agent. (This must be a street address.) O.C.G.A. 14-2-202(a)(3)

VI.   DOCUMENT CHECK-OFF LIST. This is the attachment check-off list. Verify and check off each item before filing. The Secretary of State's examiner will verify each document. NOTE: Filing corporate documents with the county office of the Clerk of Superior Court is no longer required.

VII. APPLICANT'S NAME. List the name of the applicant or filing attorney. The Secretary of State will mail the filing certificate to this address. Unless a delayed effective date is specified, corporate existence begins when the articles are filed with the Secretary of State. O.C.G.A. 14-2-203

DOCUMENT ORDER. Sign and date form and place documents in the following order for filing with the Secretary of State:

A.   Form A100—Corporate Information Form with Secretary of State fee (check) attached. (Cover letter not required.)
B.   Original Articles of Incorporation.
C.   One copy of Articles of Incorporation.

PROFIT   PROFIT

THIS IS NOT A FORM. USE ONLY AS A GUIDE.

SAMPLE FORMAT
(Please Type)

ARTICLES OF INCORPORATION

OF

_____

I.

The name of the corporation is " _____ ".

II.

The number of shares the corporation is authorized to issue is _____ .

III.

The street address of the initial registered office of the corporation is _____
and the initial registered agent of the corporation at such address is _____ .
(Include street and number, city, county, state and zip code.)

IV.

The name and address of each incorporator is: _____ .

V.

The mailing address of the initial principal office of the corporation is _____ .

IN WITNESS WHEREOF, the undersigned has executed these Articles of Incorporation.

This _____ day of _____ , 19 ____.   _____
                                                         (Name of Incorporator or Authorized Director Officer)

NOTE: In addition to the mandatory information set out above, other items as provided in O.C.G.A. §14-2-202 may be included in a corporation's articles of incorporation.

NONPROFIT   NONPROFIT

THIS IS NOT A FORM. USE ONLY AS A GUIDE.
(Please Type)

SAMPLE FORMAT
ARTICLES OF INCORPORATION
OF

_____

I.

The name of the corporation is " _____ ".

II.

The corporation is organized pursuant to the provisions of the Georgia Non-Profit Corporation Code.

III.

The corporation shall have perpetual duration.

IV.

The corporation is a non-profit corporation and is organized for the following purposes:
(state the specific purposes for which the corporation will be organized and include the general purpose clause, shown below)
to engage in any lawful business or activities related thereto; and to engage in any lawful act or activity for which corporations may be organized under the Georgia Non-Profit Corporation Code.

V.

State the manner in which the directors shall be elected or appointed. In lieu thereof, the articles of incorporation may provide that the method of election of directors be left to the bylaws.

VI.

State any provision, not inconsistent with the Corporation Code or with any other law, limiting in any manner the corporate powers conferred by this Code.

VII.

The address of the initial registered office of the corporation is _____ ,
and the initial registered agent of the corporation at such address is _____ .
(Include street and number, city, county and zip code.)

VIII.

The initial board of directors shall consist of three members, the name and address of each of which is as follows:

IX.

The name and address of the incorporator(s) is:
IN WITNESS WHEREOF, the undersigned incorporator(s) has (have) executed these Articles of Incorporation this

_____ day of _____ , 19____ .   _____

                                                         (Name of Incorporator or Representative)

The articles of incorporation may, as a matter of election, also set forth:

(1) Any provisions, not inconsistent with law, for the regulation of the internal affairs of the corporation, including, without limitation, provisions with respect to the relative rights or interest of the members as among themselves or in the property of the corporation; the manner of termination of membership in the corporation; the rights, upon such termination, of the corporation, the terminated member and the remaining members; the transferability or nontransferability of membership; and the distribution of assets on dissolution or final liquidation.
(2) If the corporation is to have one or more classes of members, any provision designating the class or classes of members and stating the qualifications and rights of the members of each class.
(3) The names of any persons or the designations of any groups of persons who are to be the initial members.
(4) A provision to the effect that the corporation shall be subordinate to and subject to the authority of any head or national association, lodge, order, beneficial association, fraternal or beneficial society, foundation, federation or other nonprofit corporation, society, organization or association.
(5) Any provision which under the Corporation Code is required or permitted to be set forth in the bylaws; any such provision set forth in the articles of incorporation need not be set forth in the bylaws.

It shall not be necessary to set forth in the articles of incorporation any of the corporate powers enumerated in Section 14-3-21, Official Code of Georgia Annotated.

S A M P L E   F O R M A T

***DO NOT RETURN TO SECRETARY OF STATE**

NOTICE OF INTENT TO INCORPORATE

Dear Sirs:

You are requested to publish twice a notice in the following form:

Notice is given that Articles of Incorporation which will incorporate (Name of Corporation) will be delivered to the Secretary of State for filing in accordance with the Georgia Business Corporation Code. (O.C.G.A. §14-2-201.1)

The initial registered office of the corporation will be located at (Address of Registered Office) and its initial registered agent(s) at such address is (Name of Registered Agent or Agents).

Enclosed is a check, draft or money order in the amount of $40.00 in payment of the cost of publishing this notice.

Sincerely,

(Name and address of
Incorporator)

rev. 7/89

S A M P L E   F O R M A T

Pitfall 9
Missing your
target market

A retail store sells to the wrong market

BARRY KNEW MEN'S FASHIONS. HE ALSO KNEW THE FLORIDA MARKET. HE HAD BEEN selling to south Florida retailers for eight years. His customers were department stores, specialty shops, and golf pro shops.

It was a special market. The colors were livelier and the styles more casual. He was often chided by his fellow salespeople from other parts of the country about the peculiarities of his market. Plaids, stripes, and paisley prints in pastel or shocking colors is what sold in his accounts. If he sold a store dark colors or a conservative look, the merchandise would sit for months. The stylishly dressed men of the area wanted the look of golf, tennis, or tropical living, and what made Barry a successful salesman, was that he knew what sold. He could sense the needs of the marketplace.

When a promising retail opportunity became available in central Florida's Brevard County, *The Space Coast*, he jumped at it. Confident that his successful wholesale selling experience would carryover into retailing, he signed a lease to be the only men's store in a 50 store enclosed mall. The community of 40,000 was starved for a man's specialty store—it had none. It was a coastal town with an abundance of golf courses.

Getting off the selling road sounded great to Barry and his family. They moved to their new community and bought a home.

Purchasing the initial inventory for the 2,000 square foot specialty store was a breeze. Barry travelled to the apparel mart with a $25,000 open to buy and placed the following orders:

fixtures and equipment	$ 6300
casual slacks and shirts	3400
dress slacks and shirts	1700
sweaters	700

belts and accessories	1225
sports coats	3700
suits	5000
ties, socks	2850
total	$25075

Approximately 80 percent of the casual wear carried the Florida resort look. There was some representation for the conservative customer, but not enough to make a complete showing. The sports coats and suits were in light colors. Accessories such as the ties were in line with the casual theme of the store's merchandise.

The store opening was a major disappointment. Instead of compliments, there was snickering and fun was poked at Barry's selection. He was shocked and confused as to the problem. Within a few weeks, Barry didn't even have the curiosity shopper. He went to the local banker for an answer.

"Barry, I've lived here all of my life. This community is unlike any other in Florida. Until the Kennedy Space Center, we were basically a fishing community of 7,000 people. Now we are 7,000 people plus 15,000 engineers and their families. Engineers are not ordinarily lively dressers. They go to work in a white shirt and plain slacks and skirts. We have no convention visitors and not much in the way of long-stay tourist because the space center owns the beach. Most of our residents look a little out of place on the golf course in their conservative attire. We are a far cry from Palm Beach."

Barry swallowed hard. He had made presumptions without taking the time to learn his target market.

Determining your target market

The song "Looking For Love In All the Wrong Places" can be paraphrased for Barry as "Looking For Sales In All the Wrong Places." Barry worked on the presumption that what worked in south Florida would certainly work in central Florida. He did not know the essence of target marketing.

Target marketing refers to breaking down the overall market for a good or service to the segment that utilizes it the most. It should be as specific as possible for the small business. Properly identifying the target determines the location, the marketing plan, and the product mix of the seller.

Barry confirmed that there was an underserved market to support his endeavor, however, he missed the mark on determining what product was needed. He might have determined his target market was men, ages 32 to 45, married, 14 years of education, and an above average per capita income level. This would have all held true for his new community, but he did not inquire as to the life-style of his market. This is termed as *psychographics*. If the target life-style for the market was professional or up and coming businessmen with leisure time, who were socially oriented, it would not apply to the Brevard County engineering community. By turning his attention to meet the needs of the engineering community, he might still be successful. His merchandise assortment will have to become more conservative to match the marketplace. Engineers need clothes, but not for the same needs as the males in south Florida.

In determining your target market, write out a description of whom you see as your prime customer. Age, income, education level, sex, marital status, hobbies, and life-style should all be addressed. This person is at the center of your target. Although you will attract customers from outside this description, the target customer is your bread and butter. Once you have identified your customer, make sure your product fulfills his or her's unsatisfied wants. *Wants* is better terminology to apply than needs, because, in most cases, it is the motivation you will stimulate. *Needs* refers to essentials for living, a very small percentage of purchases. Most of us call our wants, needs as a means of rationalizing our expenditures. Your goal is to determine the wants of your market and then act to satisfy them.

Your target market should take the form of the target shown in Fig. 9–1. The bull's-eye is the prime customer. The outer rings are the perimeter of customers you will be able to attract if the business does not limit itself.

The inner ring is the perfect customer. This needs to be highlighted. It must never be forgotten in the planning process, because it represents the bread and butter of the business. We use this customer in our approach to the market in location selection, sales forecasting, and advertising. Because advertising capital is

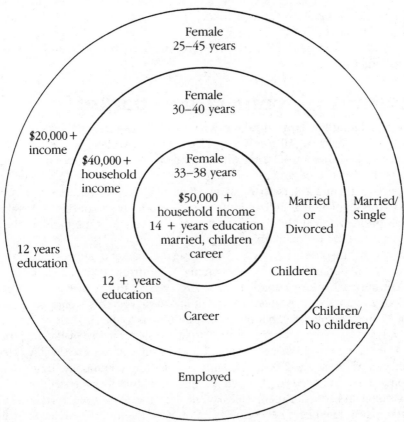

Fig. 9–1. A market profile.

usually limited, it must be aimed directly at the bull's-eye of the market. This does not mean there will not be any overlap, however. A ladies fashion store might aim for the career women between the ages of 25 and 34 but does not necessarily ignore the 40- or 22-year-old. A certain portion of the outer ring market will respond to the same marketing stimulus as the bull's-eye market. In choosing your market, follow these steps.

1. Check industry sources such as newsletters, magazines, and trade journals for prime customer identification.

2. Research the market area for representation of this prime market. This will include a demographic (population) study and a psycnographic (life-style) study.

3. Test your theories of the market. For example, selling old comic books has three markets, collectors, children, and hobbyists. An advertising test should be run for each market in order to see where your prime market is.

4. Write a customer description similar to the one shown in Fig. 9–2.

Expanding your target market

Once you have entered the market, you must concentrate on keeping your prime market while expanding to the outer market whenever feasible. Keep tabs on the

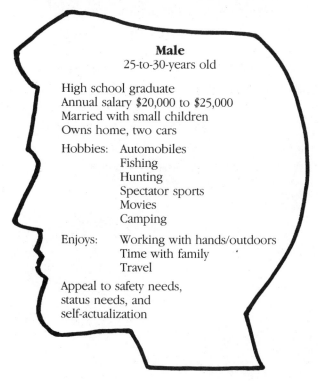

Fig. 9–2. A customer profile.

market as it changes. You will lose some customers for reasons you cannot always control, but a good marketer always has a plan to replace lost business. It is similar to inventory control, where there must be replacements available. A lost customer turns into a potential new customer. Don't drop old customers. You never know when the needs that originally made them customers will return. Learn to look at customers as to their total value over the lifetime of the business. If a customer spends $500 per year, his or her value is $10,000 over a 20-year period. If you lose that customer for three years and then get them back, their total value is still worth $8,500 (17 × $500).

Pitfall #9 summary
Target market questionnaire

By answering the following 10 questions, you will begin to learn about the psychographics of your customers. Knowing how they live will allow you to effectively design your business's approach to the market in a way that appeals to the customer's unsatisfied needs.

1. What needs are being fulfilled by your product or service?
2. What segment of the market has the greatest amount of these unfulfilled needs?
3. How does this segment live that creates these needs?
4. How do these potential customers compensate if not able to fulfill their need for your product or service?
5. Do they have the financial capability to purchase what you sell?
6. Who are the leaders and trendsetters for this group?
7. What common interests do the members of this market segment share?
8. What type of environment appeals to their aesthetic sense?
9. What common values are shared by this group?
10. What common traditions are shared by this group?

Pitfall 10

Designing a layout that discourages buying

Putting the wrong departments in the wrong places

BILL AND JEANETTE LOOKED OVER THE 12,000 SQUARE FOOT EMPTY STORE THEY HAD just signed a lease to rent. Empty, it looked enormous. How would it look filled? Where should each of the departments be placed? It was a real challenge for the ambitious entrepreneurs who were combining their retail stores into a small specialty department store.

The space was rectangular in shape with two entrances. One opened into the shopping mall, the other into the parking lot. They went to work on designing the layout for the following departments:

- ladies apparel
- bridal wear
- men's fashions
- children's clothes and toys
- greeting cards and gifts
- a small restaurant
- stockroom
- offices

Jeanette was responsible for the ladies, bridal, and children's departments. Bill was concerned with the men's, greeting cards, gifts, restaurant, stockroom, and office.

There were some built-in restrictions to accommodate. A four-foot wide delivery hallway ran 30 feet to what had been the kitchen of the previous tenant, a large restaurant. Because the kitchen area was reasonably intact, it would remain where it was, therefore dictating the location of a 600 square foot cafe. Because restaurant odors and noise were a concern, it was agreed that storage and office areas should be adjacent to the kitchen. After penciling in this consideration, the two partners needed to plot the remainder of the layout from the illustrated store outline (see Fig. 10–1).

The initial decision was the most difficult. Jeanette with her ladies' fashions experience recognized the importance of having ladies apparel spread across the mall entranceway to attract the lady shopper. Bill was insistent that, because greeting cards and gifts were so highly impulsive, that they be located along the mall en-

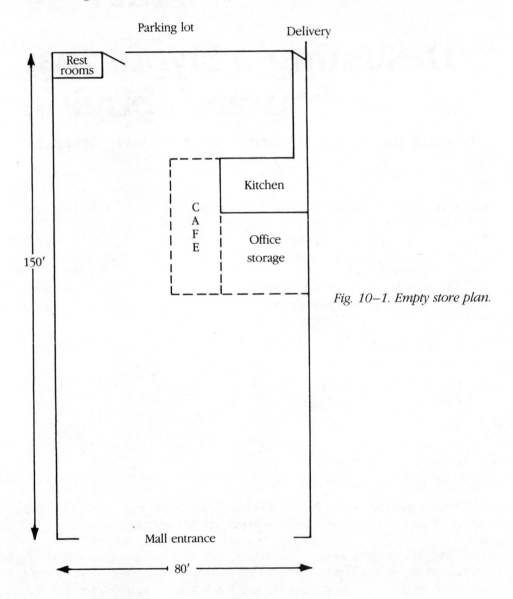

Fig. 10–1. Empty store plan.

tranceway. Both recognized that the mall entrance would certainly be used by more customers than the parking lot. The debate finally centered on what department would look the most aesthetically appealing to the walk by customer. The ladies fashions won and the greeting cards and gifts were assigned the parking lot entrance and display windows. It was decided ladies' fashions would flow into bridal wear in the front with children's clothing backing them to attract the young mothers. Men's clothes were assigned the far corner because it was the area that the partner's had the least experience with. The final plan is shown in Fig. 10–2.

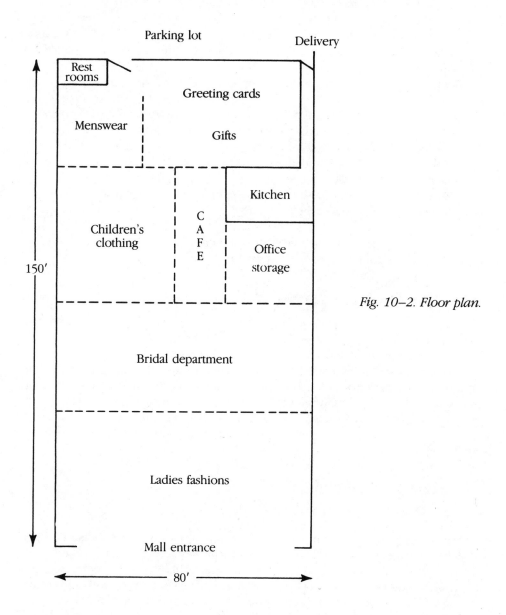

Fig. 10–2. Floor plan.

The store opened with mixed results. The ladies department performed as expected. Greeting cards and gifts seemed to hold their own during normal business activity, but seasonal sales fell far below initial projections. The restaurant was a popular addition to the merchandising concept but was not large enough to contribute to profits. The children's department, although active, was not performing in line to the amount of square feet it occupied. The men's department was a dismal failure.

Bill felt certain they were headed for doom if corrections were not made. He approached Jeanette with his ideas about realigning the store format. "Jeanette, we are losing a great amount of sales on seasonal gifts and cards simply because the walk by traffic is not reminded of the special occasions as they walk by the store. If we had this department at the front, they would be drawn into the store on every special engagement. Once in, they would be exposed to the rest of our products. It would increase the heck out of in-store traffic."

"Wait a minute, Bill, if we dismantle the fashions from the front we will look like a card and gift shop and I'll lose my biggest selling tool, the statement the displays make of looking good. Putting the clothes back towards the men's department will cause the same problems we are having with men's clothing. I don't know what it would do to bridal sales. It's not possible to have everything located in the best spot. Let's keep it like it is and keep our fingers crossed the customers will learn in time that we are the place to come for seasonal gifts and cards."

Bill went to his desk and pulled out a sheet of drafting paper to see if there was a way of showing both areas at the front. He came up with a new plan as shown in Fig. 10–3.

If he could effectively boutique off the different areas so that they appeared to be distinct shops within a store, could it work?

Design techniques

Laying out a business is a study in consumer psychology. Whether it is a complex retail structure or a simple office to sell services, the design must be tailored to please the customer in comfort, convenience, and confidence.

A professional service such as a realtor or lawyer must show an environment of confidence. A manufacturer or wholesaler must show its customer an environment of efficiency. The retailer shows warmth, security, and comfort. The objective for all is to create an environment conducive to buying. The design creates goodwill and stimulates buying. In addition, the image projected is a statement of the amount of care the entrepreneur has for the business.

Creating a conducive selling environment

A retailer should create an environment that best suits his merchandise and his clientele—environmental merchandising. The store should carry a consistent theme. If you are selling elegance, the theme should be elegant. If you are selling savings, the theme should be price promotion. The consumer enters a store with a need. By creating the right environment, you will be able to satisfy that need with a sale.

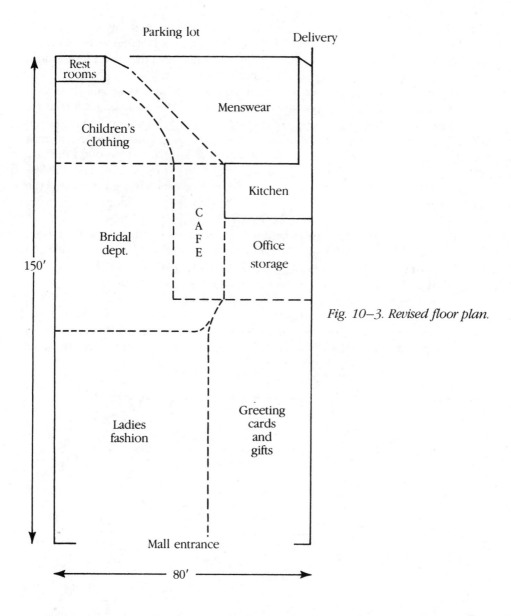

Fig. 10–3. Revised floor plan.

Needs can be stimulated by proper alignment of merchandise and displays. Proper positioning of products also allows stimulation. If you are selling a highly impulsive product, it must be situated so that it's seen and remind the customer there is a need. In Bill and Jeanette's case, they are both trying to get the space that will be seen easily in order that the customers will be reminded of their needs for clothing or a card and gift. Bill is very aware that the sight of a Valentine, Easter, or Christmas greeting card display will set in motion a reminder that there is someone the customer should remember, thus creating a need that will only be satisfied by an action. Jeanette's statement that not everything can have the most favorable space is true. What Bill is trying to do is combat the problem with a better flow of merchandise that will give better exposure and at the same time lead the customer to more selection. A properly designed plan can accomplish this goal.

Start by identifying the most important selling areas of a store and then merchandise to them. The most important area is the front right as you enter. It receives the most exposure and should be considered for highly impulsive products. The second most important area is front left as it is easily seen and convenient to turn towards. The back quadrants are used for the more specialized products that are more likely to be requested by the customer. The more planned a purchase, the less impulsive the product. Another area that can be very profitable for the retailer is the checkout area. Often, this area is surrounded by pick-up merchandise, i.e., grocery store checkout lines are dominated by candy and magazines. These products are considered point-of-purchase merchandise. The idea is to sell additional related merchandise at the same time that the consumers are reaching for their money and are in a buying mood. Point-of-purchase merchandising works and should not be overlooked. Figure 10–4 illustrates the four quadrants of a retail store.

A good design must also direct. Proper use of aisles, displays, and signs will lead customers to full exposure of the merchandise. The merchant is hopeful that the customer will see as much as possible to stimulate more needs. Wide aisles, signs at eye level, fixtures that project the merchandise towards the customers are all viable

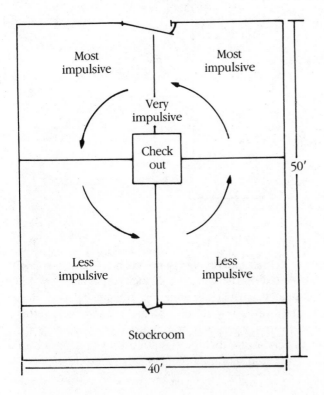

Fig. 10–4. Store quadrants.

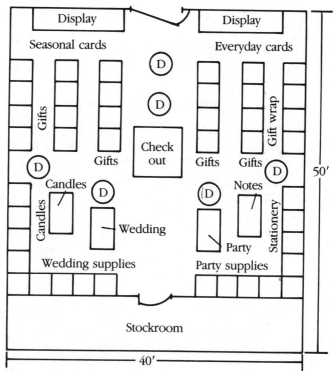

Fig. 10–5. An effective floor plan that maximizes space.

techniques. Strategically located displays will act as silent sales personnel. If displays are kept current and imaginative, they will show how the product can fulfill a need. Display locations should be drawn into the floor design to assure their effectiveness. Figure 10–5 shows a floor plan that directs traffic and uses proper display locations.

The final floor design should be very exact. It is important that all measurements are taken accurately to make sure all space is accounted for and that all fixtures fit as designed. It must show all electrical outlets and also any physical obstacles, i.e., columns, that need to be taken into account. Merchandising ideas such as effective use of colors or product groupings should also be addressed.

The design of your business is a reflection of your creativeness and can go a long way in determining your success over the competition.

Pitfall #10 summary
Business design checklist

When planning the layout of your business, make sure you include the following 10 considerations:

1. Personally take all inside measurements of space.
2. Draw an outline of fixtures to scale.

3. Note all obstacles (columns, unusual corners, etc.) and place them on the floor plan.

4. Mark off all areas for storage or auxillary use.

5. Choose colors schemes and decorating theme in consideration of target market.

6. Design lighting scheme to assure maximum exposure of product or service.

7. Draw in placement of all permanent fixturing and equipment.

8. Indicate placement of display areas and temporary placements. This is particularly important in seasonal businesses.

9. Design signing for outside and inside exposure.

10. Order carpeting, wallcoverings, fixtures, furniture, and equipment as shown in the floor plan.

Pitfall 11

Buying costly and ineffective advertising

An entrepreneur learns to get involved with his advertising

HERB ROLLINS WAS DEFINITELY DISPLEASED WITH THE RESULTS OF HIS ADVERTISING program for his RV and automobile dealership. He questioned Art Young, the sales representative for WARU-TV, at length for ideas to improve the impact.

"Art, the money I am spending and the results I am getting do not match up in any shape or form. The ads are dull—let's spice them up or else I will change media. I need some direct results."

"Herb, why don't you come down to the next taping of a new commercial and see if we can collaborate on some fresh ideas. I will line up the taping crew for 11:00 a.m. Wednesday and then we can have lunch to discuss ideas."

Herb nodded his head, "Okay, that's a deal. See you Wednesday."

Herb had always passed his thoughts about advertising to Art in meetings at the dealership. He had never attended a taping before. Perhaps it could generate some fresh insight. He arranged to have his latest deluxe RV model available at the taping, which would be held in the back lot of the studio.

When he arrived at the studio, he was introduced to Gary Albright, the spokesperson for the commercial. Art showed him the script he had written. To Herb it looked much like the same old stuff. The good looking guy standing beside the good looking vehicle touting the exceptional value available. He watched Gary through two tapings before his exasperation got the best of him.

"Hold it Art, this is the same dull stuff. Why can't there be action? Why can't Gary get excited? He has to sell, not just talk. Let me show you what I mean." With that, Herb climbed atop the RV van and shouted "I want to sell you a van." He followed with a barrage of verbiage regarding the advantages and benefits. Climbing down, the crew and cameramen applauded the creative expression. Unknowingly to Herb, they had left the cameras running.

During lunch, Art used the unedited tape to convince Herb that he should be the one to sell the products just like he had demonstrated. It took some persuasion, because Herb had never intended to be the focal point of the ad.

One week later, Herb's commercials were grabbing the attention of the entire viewing public. The impetus of the ad campaign sent sales soaring to an all-time high. The more the ads ran, the greater the sales and the greater the recognition for Herb's dealership.

Advertising planning

Herb learned an important lesson for small business owners—do it yourself. This holds true in most management functions but particularly in advertising. The owner knows more about the product than anyone else. This being the case, why should an outsider be given the responsibility of deciding how to sell it. This does not necessarily mean the owner has to appear in the television commercials or draw the newsprint ad, but it does mean that he should be very much a part of planning all advertisements and promotions. An advertisement does more than sell, it represents. It casts the image of the business. The image has been created through the eyes and actions of the owner who must then decide on that representation.

Herb was dissatisfied with the results of Art's work. What did he expect? Art knows television, he does not know RV vehicles. Only when Herb got involved did he achieve the desired results. His sitting back and letting someone control his business cost Herb a lot of money for ineffective advertising. Don't let this happen to you.

The most abused expense in a new small business is advertising. It is abused because of the lack of planning given to it and the amount of misinformation surrounding it. Small businesses survive in this country because they can offer the personalized product or service lacking in large corporations. However, in advertising the new small business owner forgets this and hops into the same arena with the large business. He insists on competing with mass media approaches to sell his product or service. Understanding advertising requires learning a few basic concepts of communication.

Communicating effectively

Being able to communicate effectively means breaking through the *noise* factors. These are the distractions that keep us from understanding, hearing, reading, seeing, or listening to a message. In advertising, they take the shape of competing and conflicting messages given to our senses. A cluttered newspaper page of ads, too many radio or television commercials screaming for attention, or a pile of ads in our mailbox are examples of "noise" distractions.

The only effective means of cutting through the noise is a continuous exposure of the ad until, through repetition, it finally gets its message through. In newspaper advertising, the only way to get proper notice is to totally dominate a page with size in a well-read section. This is very expensive and usually not affordable to the small business. The best advertising means for the small business is to directly inundate their customer by using personalized direct mail, telemarketing, or tailored presentations in the form of catalogs or brochures. This allows for singular attention to the communication. With the exception of general appeal announcements, such as the grand opening, most small businesses should stay away from mass media advertising and use their ad budgets to reach their specific target market directly.

Advertising consistency

Consistency in advertising makes efficient advertising. Too often, small business advertisers jump in and out of advertising as they feel necessary. An example would be the retailer who advertises during the fall and Christmas season but not at all during the summer months. In an approach like this, the owner has taken the name and product from the customer's world to save money but might be giving the competition an ideal time to steal his business. Although certain times of the year should get more emphasis, an advertising budget needs to be spread throughout the year to assure a consistent and well-planned program. A good program will follow a calendar similar to the one shown in Fig. 11–1.

Advertising life cycles

You must understand where your business lies on the advertising life cycle (see Fig. 11–2). Depending on whether you are in the introductory, growth, maturity, or decline stage determine the best strategy to use. If you have recently entered the market, you are in the introductory or pioneer stage. As such, your prime objective is to become discovered by your customer base. You will emphasize "new," or "now open," or "come by and see." In this stage, you might try using affordable mass media because you must be very broad in your initial approach.

As you pass into the growth stage, where your objective is to grab market share from the competition, the emphasis changes to one of declaring the features, benefits, and advantages of your business. Terminology such as "quality service" and "best prices" are often used. Because this stage is quite competitive, you should check and evaluate how your competition is advertising before determining your strategy. Whatever they are doing you will have to do better. This is normally the time you should be trying to reach your market on a personal and direct basis whenever possible.

Through this stage, your advertising should be strictly product advertising. Product advertising deals specifically with why the customer needs and should buy the product or service. The other type of advertising is institutional, directed towards the benefits and value of dealing with a particular business. As your business moves into the maturity stage, the objective will be to maintain market share. One method will be to remind the customers of your fine reputation and the stability of your business as opposed to the new market entries. This stage should combine product and institutional advertising. Ads should be specifically and personally directed towards your client base.

Dates To Remember

JANUARY

13-16   WHITE SALE

20-21   SIDEWALK SALE

FEBRUARY

14 -   VALENTINE

20 -   PRESIDENT'S DAY SALE

MARCH

17 -   ST PAT PROMOTION

15-24 -   EASTER PROMOTION

APRIL

8 -   MOONLIGHT MADNESS SALE

19 -   ANNIVERSARY SALE

MAY

20 -   Mother's DAY

24 -   LAUNCH WEDDING PROMOTION

JUNE

10 -   BRIDAL FASHION SHOW

19 -   FATHER'S DAY

JULY

14-15   SIDEWALK SALE

AUGUST

15.30   BACK to School PROMOTION
       F

SEPTEMBER

10 -   MOONLIGHT MADNESS SALE

OCTOBER

9 -   COLUMBUS DAY SALE

31 -   HALLOWEEN

NOVEMBER

20 -   LAUNCH XMAS PROGRAM

23 -   Thanksgiving

30 -   PRE-XMAS SALE

DECEMBER

7 -   XMAS OPEN HOUSE

26 -   AFTER XMAS SALE

Fig. 11–1. Advertising calendar.

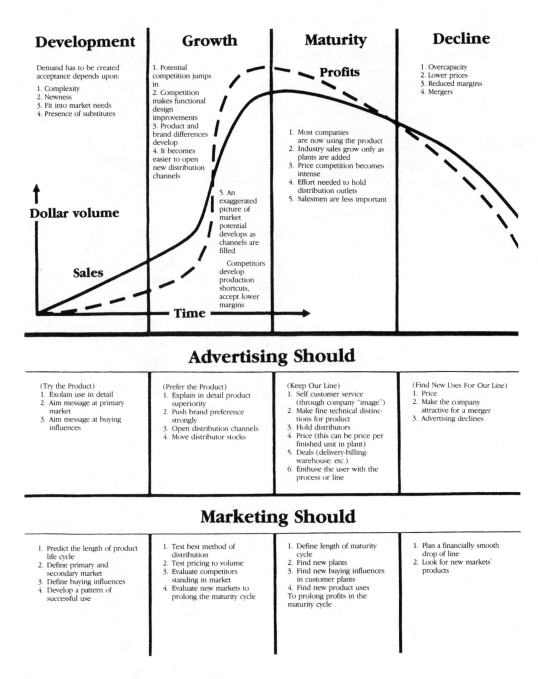

Development

Demand has to be created acceptance depends upon:

1. Complexity
2. Newness
3. Fit into market needs
4. Presence of substitutes

↑

Dollar volume

Sales

Time

Growth

1. Potential competition jumps in
2. Competition makes functional design improvements
3. Product and brand differences develop
4. It becomes easier to open new distribution channels

5. An exaggerated picture of market potential develops as channels are filled

Competitors develop production shortcuts, accept lower margins

Profits

Maturity

1. Most companies are now using the product
2. Industry sales grow only as plants are added
3. Price competition becomes intense
4. Effort needed to hold distribution outlets
5. Salesmen are less important

Decline

1. Overcapacity
2. Lower prices
3. Reduced margins
4. Mergers

Advertising Should

(Try the Product)
1. Exolain use in detail
2. Aim message at primary market
3. Aim message at buying influences

(Prefer the Product)
1. Explain in detail product superiority
2. Push brand preference strongly
3. Open distribution channels
4. Move distributor stocks

(Keep Our Line)
1. Self customer service (through company "image")
2. Make fine technical distinctions for product
3. Hold distributors
4. Price (this can be price per finished unit in plant)
5. Deals (delivery-billing-warehouse. etc.)
6. Enthuse the user with the process or line

(Find New Uses For Our Line)
1. Price
2. Make the company attractive for a merger
3. Advertising declines

Marketing Should

1. Predict the length of product life cycle
2. Define primary and secondary market
3. Define buying influences
4. Develop a pattern of successful use

1. Test best method of distribution
2. Test pricing to volume
3. Evaluate competitors standing in market
4. Evaluate new markets to prolong the maturity cycle

1. Define length of maturity cycle
2. Find new plants
3. Find new buying influences in customer plants
4. Find new product uses
To prolong profits in the maturity cycle

1. Plan a financially smooth drop of line
2. Look for new markets' products

Fig. 11–2. Advertising life cycle.

When a business starts to decline, either because of technology obsolescence or the unexpected market entry of a substitute product, the advertising thrust must be aimed at maintaining the status quo as long as possible until a new direction or plan can be put into action. This stage relies heavily on institutional advertising.

Once you decide on a new plan, the advertising will enter the cycle again. This ongoing spiral action holds true for product innovation and introduction as well.

Owner participation

As evidenced by the case in the beginning of this chapter, the owner should be involved in the planning and the presentation of the ads. You will represent the business to the public and should be scrutinized closely to make sure the proper image is transmitted. The owner knows the product and the customer the best and should be fully involved in this important selling technique. The idea should be put together at the owner's desk and then reviewed by the experts and associates. It is not difficult to create advertising copy. Keep in mind the four letters that guide advertising creators, AIDA. The *A* stands for the *Attention* all advertising must have to

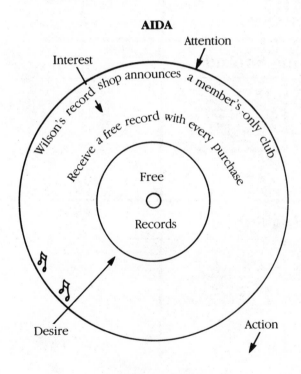

Fig. 11–3. This ad has AIDA.

Come in and register
today
Wilson's Records
Springfield Mall
Highway 405
843-1121

_____ **Table 11–1.** _____
Starch Survey

Size of ad	Women		Men	
	Noted	Read most	Noted	Read most
1 page or more	48%	19%	34%	11%
³/₄ to 1 page	43%	13%	30%	8%
¹/₂ to ³/₄	36%	10%	31%	9%
¹/₄ to ¹/₂	29%	10%	22%	7%
¹/₈ to ¹/₄	28%	10%	20%	7%
under ¹/₈	15%	5%	13%	5%
Total	31%	11%	24%	7%

get noticed. The *I* is for the *Interest* that needs to be there if you are expecting the potential customer to continue reading, listening, or viewing the advertisement. The *D* is for the *Desire* that you hope to arouse for what you are selling. The *A* stands for the *Action* you want the potential customer to take, i.e., "Buy now," or "Come in today." (See Fig. 11–3.) In planning an ad, write these four letters down and make sure all elements are present in the idea that you create. You do not need to be an artist or an audio or video technician for this. The professionals can take over from there in making the ad come alive.

Finally, evaluate your advertisements for effectiveness. This is not as simple as looking at sales volume increases because many ad campaigns will have a longer duration. Allowances must be given also to the exposure value of a business that does not show up immediately in the cash register. Although it sounds oversimplified, the best way is to ask your customers about particular ads. A good ad will be noticed and remembered while a poor one will be neither. Table 11–1 shows the difficulty in being noticed in newsprint advertising.

Pitfall #11 summary
Analyzing an advertisement

Examine the advertisement on page 96 for the AIDA features. The answer is listed below the ad.

sale spring sale spring

save on elegant diamond jewelry

20% off

We've slashed the price on every diamond in our Fine Jewelry department. Beautiful investments now irresistibly priced: earrings, bracelets, rings, and pendants. Some pieces feature luxurious rubies, emeralds, or sapphires, and all are set in 14K gold. All weights are total. Hurry in for best selection. Shown is only a sampling of the values. Fine Jewelry, D79, all Davison's. Sorry, no mail or phone orders.

	reg.	sale
A. Earstuds, ½ ct. of dias.	$795	$629
B. 14K gold hoops, 2/10 ct. of dias.	575	459
C. Loveknot earstuds, dias. centers	350	279
D. Emerald cluster ring, .56 ct. of dias.	1325	1059
E. 2/10 ct. dia. pendant	350	279
F. Ruby cluster pendant, .16 ct. of dias.	750	599
G. Earstuds, 1/10 ct. dias.	150	119
H. Emerald & dia. band ring	350	279
J. Band ring, .18 ct. dias.	375	299
K. Contemporary ring, .13 ct. of diamonds	450	359
L. Sapphire ring, 2 dias.	495	389
M. Ruby ring, .35 ct. dias.	625	499
N. 1 ct. dia. cluster ring	1850	1479
P. Contemporary ring, .24 ct. of dias.	575	459
Q. Contemporary ring, .42 ct. of dias.	1150	919
R. Cluster ring, 1 ct. of dias.	1775	1419
S. Bracelet, dias. & colored stones	350	279
Ring on hand: Wedding band. 2/10 ct. of dias.	875	699
Pendant on hand: ⅓ ct. dia. heart pendant	750	599
Bracelet on hand: rope bracelet, 3/10 ct. of dias.	1150	919

Illustration enlarged to show detail

davison's

shop suburban stores sunday 12:30 to 5:30, downtown closed

A—Sale   I—Spring, 20% off   D—Photograph   A—Shop

Pitfall 12

Using inappropriate selling techniques

The high-pressure selling philosophy that backfired

GEORGE WAS DISAPPOINTED IN THE SALES REPORTS LAYING ON HIS DESK. ALL THREE of his salespeople were performing below expectations. Although the number of sales calls had increased, the dollar results were below the previous quarter. He wondered whether the new sales strategy he had introduced four months ago was backfiring.

The new strategy was the result of George being impressed by a speaker he had heard at a convention. The speaker discussed "selling to the max" in a very motivational presentation. The theme was one of not relenting when selling. His philosophy was the more you ask for, the more you sell. The lesson was not to give up and not to take no for an answer. Persistence pays off.

The timing of the speech was appropriate, as the packaging industry was in the throes of a slump. The healthy sales increases over the past five years had come to a screeching halt for George and for most of the industry. It seemed everyone was grasping for an answer to the slowdown. George had been pondering ways to get more from his sales force. They too had been disappointed as their commissions had become stagnant. Maybe, thought George, we need to push harder.

In presenting the new sales philosophy to the sales force, George received a lukewarm response. His plan was to increase the number of calls per clients, offer price reductions for immediate delivery of certain size orders, and remind clients of the expense of handling small orders. From the results on his desk it was apparent it wasn't working. He called in Fred Wilson, his top salesperson, for some feedback.

"George, I feel like a used car salesman at times and a hatchet man at other times. I am not used to selling deals. I am used to selling pride in product. I am also very hesitant to infer that we might not be able to accept such small orders. Some of our small accounts will gladly tell you how much their small orders have added up over the years. Add to that the extra sales calls and it is apparent we are gaining resentment, not sales."

George knew Fred was right. What had he been thinking?

Understanding your customer's needs

George needs to go back and review some of the basic selling principles. He must sell to the customer's needs, not his. He has panicked into a situation that can do irreparable harm if not corrected.

The sales philosophy of a business must fit the type of clientele of that particular business. Certainly, selling automobiles uses a far different approach than selling stocks and bonds. Furthermore, selling Cadillacs differs from selling Chevrolets, as does selling penny stocks differs from selling blue chip bonds. Proper selling is based on satisfying the particular needs, or wants, of the customer. The starting point of arriving at a sales philosophy is determining what needs the product is intended to satisfy.

Your customers needs should be addressed in the description of your target market (see chapter 9). Determine whether your product is satisfying basic physiological needs (food, water), safety (shelter, protection), or more advanced human needs such as belonging and love, self esteem, or self actualization. The psychologist Dr. Abraham Maslow in his theory of the hierarchy of human needs, developed these need levels years ago and they still hold great relevancy in marketing theory today. By determining if your customer is buying a product in order to feel good about themselves, to make an impression on others, or to assure their survival economically or physically, allows you to devise a sales strategy that aims at satisfying and relieving the tension created by an unfulfilled need. Before buying, consumers go through a four-step process:

1. They perceive a need. This need creates a tension from within.
2. They decide to relieve the tension by acting to fulfill the need.
3. They decide what and whose product or service has the highest probability of fulfilling their need or solving their problem.
4. Influenced by the effective presentation of your product or service, they decide to buy from you.

In selling to the consumer market, you should determine in what area of the consumer life cycle your target customer falls. Use Table 12–1 to help you locate your customer.

Finding where your consumer lies in the life cycle helps determine the consumer's purchasing power and identifies the needs you are selling to. It should be used in describing your target market.

Sales training ingredients

Once you understand your customer's psychological and need profile, you will be able to design an effective selling plan centered around the features, advantages, and

_____ **Table 12–1.** _____
Consumer Life Cycle

Stage In Life Cycle	Buying Behavior Pattern
Single, no children	Few financial burdens. Fashion leaders, recreation oriented.
Newly married, no children	Highest purchase rate. Cars, refrigerators, furniture.
Full nest I: youngest under 6	Home purchasing at peak. Baby needs, washers, dryers, etc.
Full nest II: youngest child over 6	Financial position better. Both spouses often working. Buy large packages/ quantities.
Full nest III: older couples with dependent children	Financial position still better. Hard to influence with advertising.
Empty nest I: older couples, no children at home	Home ownership at peak. Not interested in new products.
Empty nest II: older couples	Drop in income. Stay home, buy medical care products.
Solitary survivor, in labor force	Income good, but likely to stay home.
Solitary survivor, retired	Drop in income, medical needs.

benefits of your product and how they satisfy those needs. This requires product knowledge on behalf of all those selling. Good selling comes from believing that what you are selling is good for the buyer. A good salesperson is persuasive and knowledgeable about the product and also about the company she represents. She must have the confidence that what she is selling will be backed up by the organization. She must know all policies, procedures, and rules that affect her ability and authority to properly execute a sale.

As the owner, it is your responsibility to properly prepare your sales force. Sales training does not necessarily require elaborate or expensive programs. What it does require is consistency and follow up. Good sales training motivates and educates. It stimulates the desire to succeed and educates the sales force about the product and the company. Motivation will decline, however, if not reinforced, as will education become stagnant if not brought up to date. Therefore, your sales training efforts should follow a regular timetable. Whether you decide it's daily, weekly, or monthly, you must follow through with a consistent program and format. Equip your salespeople with the following information:

A proper approach.   Any sales approach must gain attention, stimulate interest, and provide a transition into an effective presentation. The approach might be a statement concerning a benefit of the product, a demonstration of the product, or a question aimed at discovering or uncovering a need or problem that can be satisfied with the purchase.

A professional presentation.   A good presentation will discuss the features, advantages, and benefits of the product. Its objective is to create a desire, develop a positive attitude, and instill a belief in what you are selling. A good presentation persuades, builds trust, asks for participation, and proves statements.

A method of handling objections.   A good salesperson can properly antici-pate objections. He can turn them into a question that will give them further reason to buy. It is important to be able to identify the real objection. The most prominent objection is cost, although it might be disguised as stalling. Other objections include design or color. Handle objections as they arise, but don't ignore or put them off.

An effective technique to close a sale.   Closing a sale should be thought of as helping the customer make a decision that will benefit them. There are many closing techniques, however, all of them require that the salesperson ask for an order. The salesperson should feel personally comfortable with a closing technique and be prepared to employ it regardless of the number of objections.

A proper follow-up program.   Your salespeople must understand the im-portance of the last impression as well as the first impression. Leaving the customer with a favorable impression creates goodwill and generates future sales. Your busi-ness is dependent on repeat sales. Repeat sales come through buyer confidence in your product and your service. Whether it is as simple as a retail salesclerk compli-menting a customer on their choice of selection or a realtor sending flowers to a new homeowner, good follow up must be a regular part of your sales program.

Finally, keep on top of your sales force's progress. Remind them of the impor-tance of leaving a favorable impression, whether they are successful or not in the sales call. It is as important to retain customers as it is to gain new customers.

Pitfall #12 summary
The 10-step selling process

In training your sales personnel, make sure they learn all of the following steps of the sales process. These 10 steps should be addressed as they relate to your product or service.

1. Prospecting: Locate and qualify prospects.
2. Preapproach: Obtain appointment or interview, determine the sales objec-tive, develop a customer profile, determine needs, and prepare a strategy.
3. The approach: Meet the prospect and introduce the sales presentation.
4. The presentation: Address features, advantages, and benefits by using proof statements, visual aids, demonstrations, and dramatizations. Continue to un-cover needs.
5. The trial close: Ask for opinions during presentation.
6. The objections: Uncover hidden and open objections.
7. Meet the objections: Answer objections completely.
8. Trial close again: Ask opinion after answering each objection.
9. The close: Entice the prospect to the conclusion to buy.
10. The follow up: Service the customer after the sale.

Pitfall 13

Setting prices that hold down profits

Competing with a discount

"DARN, BUSINESS STINKS. SALES ARE FLAT, PROFITS ARE FLAT, WE'RE NOT MAKING ANY progress. We have got to do something." Jack pounded his fist on the desk, totally frustrated. For three years he had done everything possible to get his men's clothing store to a profitable level. He had succeeded by showing a small profit the past year, but now was watching helplessly as sales and profits slipped. He was hoping this meeting with his assistant manager, Paul, could create a plan.

"Jack, the discounters are killing us. In the past year, the specialty store discount chain opened in the mall and the mass merchandiser discount house opened across town. They are basically selling what we sell at 20 to 40 percent less. We are going to have to meet those prices to survive."

"But Paul, it's been hard enough to make a profit with a 50 percent retail markup, how can we do it on less? How much more would we have to sell? Hand me a pad and let me see if I can figure it out."

Jack started by looking at the past year's income statement.

Sales	$300,000
less cost of goods	− 160,000
Gross profit	140,000
less operating expenses	− 120,000
Net operating profit	$20,000

Knowing that his average sale was $50, he figured his customer count to be 6,000 transactions.(6000 × $50 = $300,000) Using these figures as his base, he first calculated that if he reduced the average price by 20 percent from $50 to $40, he would sell 20 percent more transactions, 7,200 transactions instead of 6,000. His projection was as follows:

Sales	$288,000	
less cost of goods	− 190,000	(7200 × $25 plus freight per unit)
Gross profit	98,000	
less operating expenses	− 125,000	
Net operating loss	(27,000)	

That sure wouldn't work. The percentage rise in cost of goods to purchase the extra units at the same price would not be offset by selling at the reduced price. In addition, his operating expenses would rise somewhat to accommodate the extra customers. So what would happen if the 20 percent price reduction would double the unit sales?

Sales	$480,000	(12,000 transactions × $40 ave. sale)
Less cost of goods	− 310,00	(12,000 × $25 plus freight)
Gross profit	$ 170,000	
Less oper expenses	− 150,000	
Net operating profit	$ 20,000	

That's just fine thought Jack. Double my investment, double my risk, just to get to where I am now. I don't even have the space to accommodate that much volume. There must be a better way.

Protecting your profit margin

There is a better way. Small businesses cannot take on the discounters without great surpluses of risk capital. They shouldn't have to. The small business advantage never has been in price, it has always been in service. Jack needs to recognize the only weapon in his arsenal is better and more personalized service to the customer. This is a bonus the specialty store shopper will pay for.

It is imperative that the owner protect the gross margin price on his goods. If you make a $100 sale, it might break down as follows:

Sale	$ 100
Cost of good	− 50
Freight	− 4
Gross profit	$ 46

Less operating expenses per dollar of revenue:

Rent	− $10
Payroll	− 10
Utilities	− 3
Insurance	− 2
Advertising	− 3
Supplies	− 2
Other	− 2
Net profit	$14

If there is any debt, it is paid from the $14. Therefore, in a good situation the small business owner rarely makes more than 14 percent of sales. Because the cost of sales is fixed and most operating expenses are relatively fixed, any discount from the regular markup price will more than likely come from the small profit margin. For example, a $200,000 volume operation might make a $28,000 profit, if prices drop 10 percent, sales drop $20,000 and expenses stay approximately the same. The great percentage of the $20,000 drop will come out of the owners pocket.

To add fuel to the difficulty of competing in price with large businesses, consider that the stockholders of large chains are quite satisfied with a 2 or 3 percent profit on sales of millions of dollars. In other words, you have the challenge of quadrupling the profits of large businesses with less weapons. The only way is by doing a better job of serving the customer in order that he or she feels the value received is worth the value paid.

This service might be in the form of personalizing yourself to the customer. Whether it be free, distinctive gift wrapping, fun contests, handwritten letters to announce events, special orders, free delivery, or any number of low cost extras, the idea is to let the customers know that they are appreciated and important.

Small manufacturers are often guilty of the same defensive pricing strategy. They look at the cost of the materials, but negate the cost of their time in order to gain a sale. This only works for a short time and is bound to end in disaster.

Understanding price points

It is important that the small business owner understand the concept of price points. Price points are the different plateaus of price levels that cause inhibitors to enter the mind of customers. They are in all industries at all cost levels. The customer will pay what they feel is fair for the anticipated reward or value of a good or service. This might mean $1 for a candle or $50,000 for an airplane. They have a perceived mind set as to what is an equitable price to pay. At times, this can be influenced by supply and demand or by fashion crazes, but only to a certain point. The small business owner must understand his customer and his product sufficiently to not violate price points. He also needs to know that he can use price points to his benefit.

For example, small retailers should understand that price resistance can occur in $5 intervals, i.e., a price under $10 is important, just as under $15, $20, or $25 for product acceptance. If that is understood, then it should also be understood that the range between the price points is free game. In other words, the difference between $12.50 and $13.50 is rather minimal in today's marketplace. That being the case, a price move from $12.50 to $13.50 might be totally justified while a move from $9.50 to $10.50 might be quite hazardous because you are violating a price point.

It works the same for a manufacturer. A craft manufacturer becomes obsessed with being able to wholesale their craft for $3.50 per unit in order that the retailers can put it on their shelves for $7. The cost of that unit might be materials $1.06, labor $1.60, and sales commission to the sales representative $0.52, leaving a potential profit of $0.32 per unit. That might be acceptable if everything goes perfect, but by the time returns, defects, or lost shipments are accounted for, the owner could be facing a loss situation on each unit. In his attempt to maintain a low wholesale cost, he is jeopardizing the operation. If the product is good he should realize that the retailer will be able to sell it almost as well at $9.50 than $7.50. This raises the wholesale price to $4.75. The extra dollar represents a 28 percent increase in profit margin and a 400 percent increase in profit potential return per unit. Considering this type of increased profit potential, it would be well worth the risk of losing a small percentage of units ordered in order to sell at a profitable and stable level.

The small business owner should be able to do a better job with products and services and should be entitled to receive added value for his efforts.

Pitfall #13 summary
Where the money goes by industry

The following charts show the percent of expenses to receipts paid out to the various operating components of businesses by industry classification. The classifications are as follows:

FIRE—Financial, Insurance, Real Estate
Comm—communication
Serv—Services
Tran—Transportation
EGS—Electrical, Gas, and Sanitary Services
Tot—Total
Mfg—Manufacturing
Ag—Agriculture—Mining
ReTr—Retail Trade
Con—Construction
WhTr—Wholesale Trade

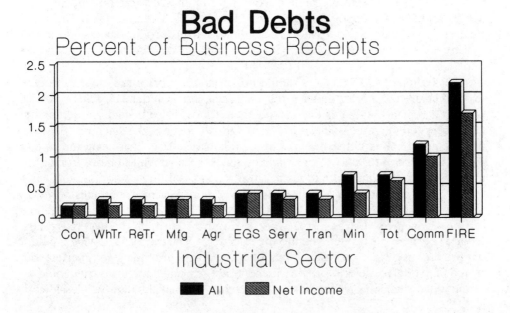

Interest Paid

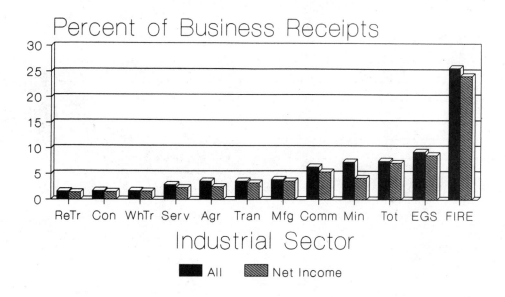

Rent on Business Property

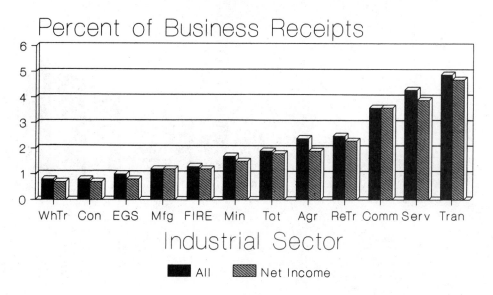

Taxes (Excluding Federal)

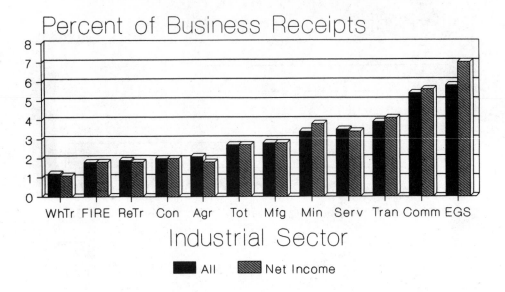

Other Expenses

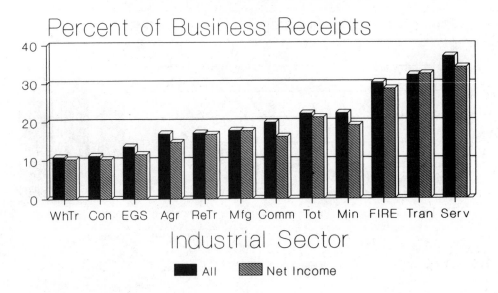

Repairs

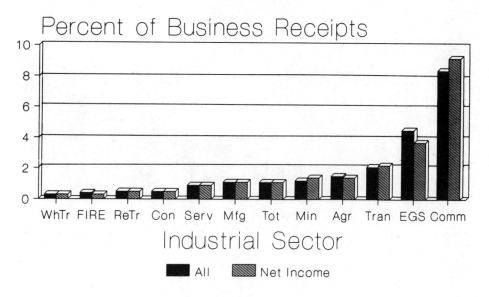

Advertising

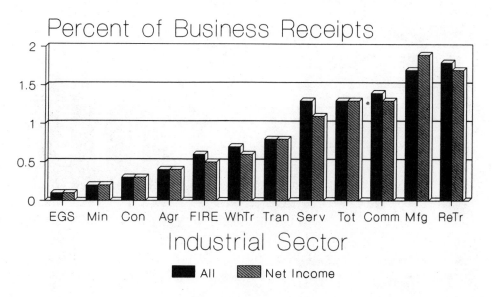

Pensions & Other Benefits

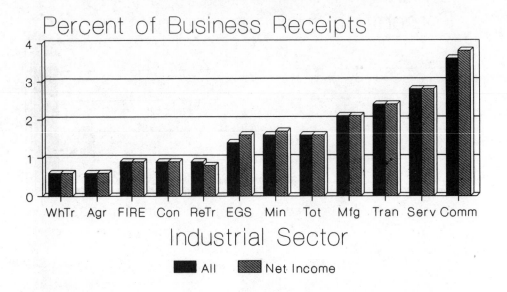

Depreciation, Depl, Amortization

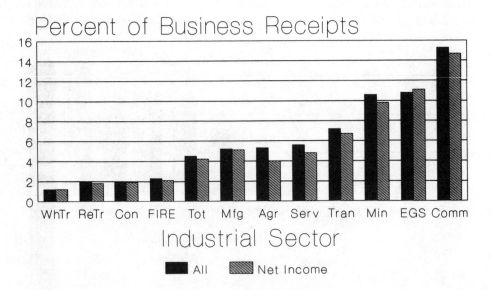

Compensation of Officers

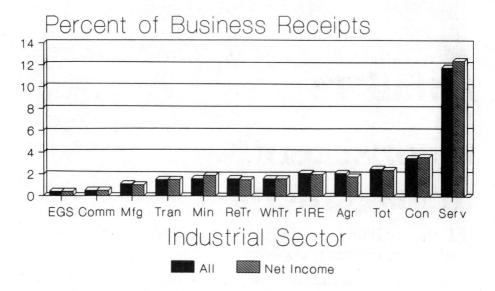

Percent of Business Receipts

Industrial Sector

Pitfall 14

Inconsistent management

The inconsistent manager who spends double on training costs

"I THINK YOU WILL FIND THIS STORE A VERY ENJOYABLE PLACE TO WORK, SUSAN. WHAT we can't supply in wages we more than make up for with a cooperative and happy work environment. We are as flexible as possible in scheduling and encourage everyone to take a participative attitude. I will be your direct supervisor and I try to interfere as little as possible. Come with me, and I will introduce you to Sharon and Debbie. They will teach you the ropes."

Roger felt good about his new employee. She seemed like the type who would stay for a while, not the usual two to three months. He was anxious to get her broken in.

Susan was happy to have found a nice store to work in that was not far from home. Roger seemed sincere and she thought it was going to work out well.

Sharon and Debbie were cordial, although somewhat reserved. They taught her the cash register procedures and explained the inventory control system. After two weeks, she felt comfortable with her assignments, but still felt like an outsider with the other girls. She did learn that although, they liked the store and the customers, they were fearful of Roger's moods. Some days he was delightful, other days he was temperamental and very impulsive in his behavior.

Susan's first encounter with this occurred at the cash register as she was writing a customer refund. "Who told you to write it that way?," Roger admonished.

"Debbie," Susan answered.

"Well it is all wrong, doesn't she know anything. I'll go talk to her, meanwhile will you please pick up that paper on the floor. This place looks like a pig sty." Roger abruptly took the refund slip and went directly to Debbie and gave her a sharp reprimand in front of a customer.

An outgrowth of this incident was Susan's acceptance by the other two girls. They started complaining together about the erratic behavior of their boss. Debbie was insistent, "I will not be treated that way. When he is in one of those moods, I am getting out of his way. I'll spend my day in the stockroom or else say I am sick and leave early."

It wasn't long before Roger lost his temper at Debbie and fired her on the spot. Her replacement lasted less than two weeks before Roger fired her on one of his bad days. Sharon and Susan started searching for new jobs, because they never knew if they would be next. Susan didn't want to leave but living with such inconsistency was getting to her.

Hiring smart

Roger is learning a very expensive lesson. His inconsistent approach to employees is the cause of high turnover. High turnover adds to overhead, because it requires a constant program of retraining employees, not to mention a very poor morale situation.

The two weeks that it took Susan to feel comfortable was two weeks of not getting 100 percent employee performance. In that two weeks, there was time spent showing her the basic operations under close supervision. This requires tying up another employee from performing other duties. After this period, there was certainly a time of adjustment in which she needed assistance in the form of asking questions, finding supplies, and learning regular customers. At best, she was a slow producer.

If you consider the cost of the additional hours for someone to train her and the effect of slow production, Roger has spent the equivalent of two weeks of wages on an employee who will more than likely be gone in three months. Multiply this by four such employees over the course of a year, and it would mean eight weeks, or 320 hours, of paid wages for each new employee each year. It is an unnecessary and unaffordable expense for a small business. Personal recruitment for small business is usually handicapped by the lack of capital resources.

Personnel recruitment for the small business is normally handicapped by the lack of capital resources. It is unlikely that you will be able to compete directly with the large companies in terms of benefit programs and wages. The people you recruit might be short on experience and skills, but hopefully long on enthusiasm and determination. Most likely, they will share some of your own qualities because they also do not want to work in the large organizational structure. They are looking to be part of a group that can work for goals that they will feel part of accomplishing. The small business can offer that opportunity by creating a work environment that allows the employees to be recognized and rewarded for the future successes of the business.

Motivating your employees

A small business is a very personal environment, almost like a family. Everyone is involved with the ultimate goal of achieving profits through a better business, free from the red-tape bureacracy of a big business. People are not numbers. Employees work hand-in-hand with the owner in building success. This appeals to many people, because it is an opportunity for individual recognition for their efforts. If an owner is sincere in his offer that, if the business does well, everyone will benefit, there is even greater motivation for excellence.

At the same time, an environment of loyalty and comradery is created. A team develops that, if managed properly, will become very cohesive and perform like a properly tuned machine. This comradery fosters enthusiasm and honesty and forces the misfit out. If there is any dishonesty, it will be reported to the owner because it will represent a threat to the group and thus, the individual's profits.

So, how does the small business owner build a team that performs at 100 percent at all times? He or she should follow these suggestions.

Hire people you like

Hiring people you like is not foolproof, because the hiring decision is based on a brief exposure to the applicant, however, there are certain things to look for. There should be a good feeling of communication during the interview. Does the applicant smile when you do? Is there a feeling of attractiveness to personalities? Is there eye-to-eye contact? How do you feel about the person the day after the interview? Will the person be acceptable to the others on the team? Is there a sharing of personal values in areas such as family, philosophy, and goals?

The intent of the interview should be to explore mutual avenues of interests. Providing that you have screened the applicant for basic skills and aptitudes, the actual job performance can be taught, but many of these intangibles must be inherent if the match is to be successful.

Once all of these factors are apparent, a job offer can be made. It is important that the initial work period, or probationary period, be clearly stated so that all parties have the opportunity to evaluate the decision. This means that for a certain period, which might be as long as a month, the employee will not be required to give notice of termination nor will the employer have to feel it is necessary to follow any termination procedures. If during this period, a clear fit does not develop, the employee must be let go, regardless of his actual job performance. If a new employee causes a disruption among the team, it will snowball into a poor morale situation that will prove very costly in the long run. Also, keep in mind that if you, the boss, do not feel comfortable with an employee, the employee more than likely does not feel comfortable with you.

Flexible management

Give as many intangibles to your employees as possible. Be flexible, you are building a familylike atmosphere. If an employee needs time off to take a trip, go to school, attend a wedding, or whatever, do your best to accommodate that request. Because you cannot pay what large companies do, it is imperative that you offer what they cannot. There doesn't have to be concrete policies that state a day off must be approved two weeks in advance. As long as someone can fill in for the person, arrangements should be made to honor a request for time off.

Look around for other benefits you might provide, such as discounts on the merchandise or services that you sell. This can sometimes add up to substantial savings to the employee without costing the employer direct cash outlays. Consider having social gatherings for your team. Have them to your home or take them out for lunch or dinner. Group gatherings build comradery. Attend their special events such as weddings, graduations, baby showers, etc. You should act as the head of the family.

Including employees on business conditions

Be as honest and open about business conditions to your employees as prudently as possible. Managing a small business is a very personal experience. Because you are working with a small group of employees on a regular basis, they will have a good idea of general business conditions just by observing you, so why hide it? Sharing the successes and failures of the operation will help build loyalty and understanding. You will want them to understand why it is not possible to give a raise at certain times. Their caring about you and the goals of the business will motivate them to perform at their highest.

Offering incentives

Make working fun and competitive by offering bonus prizes or cash for good performance. There is an important difference between wages and bonuses. Wages are paid for work performance at the end of a work period. Bonuses are paid for current performance. You might be restricted on pay scales, but there should be times when you are able to offer extras for good performance. Contests to win rewards for good performance can be a lot of fun and increase morale. They are also not a commitment for the future, as are pay raises. Often, prizes are more appreciated than cash because extra cash might go to pay bills, while a prize is something that can be kept and enjoyed for a long time. One rule to follow is that everyone who participates in the contest must receive something so that no one is a loser.

Becoming a participative boss

A good boss is a participative boss. Because you act as the leader, captain, and motivator of the group, you must set the example. If you do not lean over to pick up a piece of paper on the floor, do not expect your employees to do so. People do not work for you, they work with you. Leading by participation means working side-by-side together, to achieve the common goals of the organization. The successful entrepreneur is a human resource developer, not a fire-breathing dragon forcing things to be done her way. She listens, discusses, and invites employees to participate with her in managing the functions at hand.

Pitfall #14 summary
Interview questionnaire

During an interview with a prospective employee, lead the discussion into discovering the answers to the following questions. Their answers can reveal how they feel about themselves.

1. What is the candidates family history?
2. What organizations do they feel a sense of loyalty to?
3. What are their inspirations?
4. Have they ever held a position that they felt was in conflict with their own personal values?
5. What do they do for fun?
6. What makes them laugh?
7. If faced with a personal problem, who would they most likely turn to for help?
8. What is their favorite movie or book?
9. What has been their greatest award or recognition?
10. How do they measure success?

Living off cash flow, not profits

The small business owner who lived high on the hog for a short period of time

BUSINESS WAS GOING WELL FOR BOB WALTON. DAILY CASH RECEIPTS FOR HIS NEW gift shop were approximately $700 per day, and they would grow higher as he neared the Christmas season. The checking account had a healthy balance as deposits mounted.

Bob used the first Monday of the month as the principal bill paying day. This assured him of paying all invoices by the tenth and receiving prompt pay discounts. There seemed to be ample money available as dating terms on much of the seasonal merchandise was designed to be due after the holiday. He paid himself a draw of $1,000 every other week, which he felt was the minimum he could get by on.

A year after opening, things were going so well he gave himself a handsome raise in his draw. This coincided with the purchase of a new home and shortly after, a new car. There were even a couple of nice trips with his family. He lived on a very loose personal budget that was supplemented by extra draws if things got a little tight.

Until after the second Christmas season, all bills were paid on time with discounts. At this time, there were a few he had to let go until the end of the month but he felt confident this would be corrected shortly.

A problem arose the following June when he was forced to delay approximately half of the month's invoices in order to meet a quarterly bank note obligation. Although a few creditors sent him reminder notices, Bob continued with his fast-paced life-style. More problems surfaced 90 days later when another bank payment was due. Once again, invoices were put off. More notices arrived, and some phone calls were received requesting payment.

It soon became a cycle of putting off one obligation in order to meet another. Bob fell 30 days late, then 60, then 90, with his creditors. Eventually, the vendors would ship only C.O.D. because of the tardiness. Although business remained good, it was not good enough to finance the purchase of goods in advance. The only way of raising the necessary cash was to reduce inventory, which, of course, reduced sales. The extra cash that had always been there dried up. The bottom fell out on Bob's fantasy life-style.

Using cash wisely

Bob is the victim of a very tempting mistake—using revenues, and not profits, to live on. It is very tempting because, in most businesses, there is a daily influx of cash that is available for a short period of time. Cash is not profit, however, and there must be a degree of self discipline to keep your hands out of the till.

Bob used up his allowance time that he had to pay bills. By letting the bill paying slip a week here and a week there, he created a false sense of rationalization. In a business such as his, there can be considerable money made available to the owner by doing this.

If a business takes in $300,000 per year and it pays out $150,000 for purchase of replacement inventory that averages $12,500 per month paid out in invoices. This means that $12,500 is conceivably available to the owner in extra cash if he or she decides to postpone paying the bills. Some months it might be considerably higher if it is a seasonal business that allows the payment of invoices after the season is complete.

Because most creditors will show a certain amount of patience, at least initially, the owner might not be aware of the dangerous path being followed. Unfortunately, however, it will catch up to him just as it did Bob. Once this pattern is established it will snowball into a situation so treacherous the only way out is to borrow money to survive. Borrowing money to buy assets that can increase revenues is one thing, but borrowing to pay debts is a definite no.

Allocating money correctly

Once the profit level is established, it must be the only money available for the owner. If it increases, there might be more money available, on the other hand, if it decreases, the owner must make the necessary sacrifice. In the face of mortgage payments and family expenses, it can be a difficult discipline to stick to but there is no choice. To help you allocate your money correctly, follow these guidelines:

1. For a new business, set aside three months of operating money before the doors are open. This will allow for time to make a progress check against projections. If the projections for the business are met, there will still be the equivalent of three months earnings available for the owner that can remain as a surplus in the operating account. If the projections are not met, the new owner will have to make the necessary adjustment in his anticipated earnings to reflect the difference. If done correctly, this will still allow reserve funds to be available at the new anticipated level.

2. A detailed cash flow analysis must be made that shows anticipated fluctuations of revenues. Use the cash flow plan form shown in Fig. 15–1. In a highly seasonal business, the amount of cash available will vary widely depending on the time of the year. Some choose to vary their income level according to these fluctuations. Others will put extra money from cash surplus times in a savings account to be used for owner's pay during slower times. This allows a consistent rate of pay for the owner that might prove easier to handle in regards to the family budget.

3. Do not use all of the profits for the owner's draw. In addition to owner remuneration, there must be money available to assure the long-run stability of the business. Inventory must grow with the business and equipment must be added. These additions should be paid from profits earned, not money borrowed. In addition, equipment and leasehold improvements such as carpeting will need to be replaced. The government allows you to deduct a certain percentage of these types of capital asset expenditures as depreciation. Your equipment replacement fund should be at least equal to what you deduct as depreciation expenses.

If you will discipline yourself to properly allocate your profits to all necessary areas before paying yourself, you will save yourself the worse nightmare a small business owner endures.

Pitfall #15 summary
Cash management guidelines

The following aid has been published by the Small Business Administration as a guide to the business owner on how to plan the movement of cash through the business. The prime objective for any business is to survive. That means, a firm must have enough cash to meet its obligations. This aid shows the owner-manager how to plan for the movement of cash through the business and thus plan for future requirements.

Introduction

"Business is booming. This month alone, the sales volume has risen over 50 percent."

Many proud owner-managers equate growth in sales volume with the success of their enterprise. But many of these so-called "successful" businesses are becoming insolvent because they do not have enough cash to meet the needs of an increasing sales volume. Without cash, how can the business pay its bills, meet its payroll requirements, and purchase merchandise for the increased sales demand?

A business must have enough cash to meet its legal obligations and avoid becoming insolvent. This is a primary business objective that might override other objectives, such as sales volume. What good is additional sales volume if you're out of business?

Sufficient cash is one of the keys to maintaining a successful business. Thus, you must understand how cash moves or flows through the business and how planning can remove some of the uncertainties about future requirements.

MONTHLY CASH

See Reverse Side for Instructions and Public Comment Information

NAME OF BUSINESS		ADDRESS				OWNER				

	Pre-Start-up Position		1		2		3		4		5	
YEAR MONTH	Estimate	Actual	Estimate	Actual	Estimate	Actual	Estimate	Actual	Estimate	Actual	Estimate	Actual
1. CASH ON HAND (Beginning of month)												
2. CASH RECEIPTS												
(a) Cash Sales												
(b) Collections from Credit Accounts												
(c) Loan or Other Cash injection (Specify)												
3. TOTAL CASH RECEIPTS (2a + 2b + 2c = 3)												
4. TOTAL CASH AVAILABLE (Before cash out) (1 + 3)												
5. CASH PAID OUT												
(a) Purchases (Merchandise)												
(b) Gross Wages (Excludes withdrawals)												
(c) Payroll Expenses (Taxes, etc.)												
(d) Outside Services												
(e) Supplies (Office and operating)												
(f) Repairs and Maintenance												
(g) Advertising												
(h) Car, Delivery, and Travel												
(i) Accounting and Legal												
(j) Rent												
(k) Telephone												
(l) Utilities												
(m) Insurance												
(n) Taxes (Real estate, etc.)												
(o) Interest												
(p) Other Expenses (Specify each)												
(q) Miscellaneous (Unspecified)												
(r) Subtotal												
(s) Loan Principal Payment												
(t) Capital Purchases (Specify)												
(u) Other Start-up Costs												
(v) Reserve and/or Escrow (Specify)												
(w) Owner's Withdrawal												
6. TOTAL CASH PAID OUT (Total 5a thru 5w)												
7. CASH POSITION (End of month) (4 minus 6)												
ESSENTIAL OPERATING DATA (Non-cash flow information) A. Sales Volume (Dollars)												
B. Accounts Receivable (End of month)												
C. Bad Debt (End of month)												
D. Inventory on Hand (End of month)												
E. Accounts Payable (End of month)												
F. Depreciation												

SBA FORM 1100 (1–83) REF: SOP 60 10 Previous Editions Are Obsolete

Fig. 15–1. Monthly cash flow projection worksheet.

FLOW PROJECTION

Form Approval:
OMB No. 3245–0019
Expires: 8–31–91

	TYPE OF BUSINESS				PREPARED BY				DATE	

6		7		8		9		10		11		12		TOTAL		
														Columns 1—12		
Estimate	Actual	Estimate	Actual	Estimate	Actual	Estimate	Actual	Estimate	Actual	Estimate	Actual	Estimate	Actual	Estimate	Actual	
																1.
																2.
																(a)
																(b)
																(c)
																3.
																4.
																5.
																(a)
																(b)
																(c)
																(d)
																(e)
																(f)
																(g)
																(h)
																(i)
																(j)
																(k)
																(l)
																(m)
																(n)
																(o)
																(p)
																(q)
																(r)
																(s)
																(t)
																(u)
																(v)
																(w)
																6.
																7.
																A.
																B.
																C.
																D.
																E.
																F.

GUIDELINES

GENERAL

Definition: A cash flow projection is a forecast of cash funds* a business anticipates receiving, on the one hand, and disbursing, on the other hand, throughout the course of a given span of time, and the anticipated cash position at specific times during the period being projected.

Objective: The purpose of preparing a cash flow projection is to determine deficiencies or excesses in cash from that necessary to operate the business during the time for which the projection is prepared. If deficiencies are revealed in the cash flow, financial plans **must** be altered either to provide more cash by, for example, more equity capital, loans, or increased selling prices of products, or to reduce expenditures including inventory, or allow less credit sales until a proper cash flow balance is obtained. If excesses of cash are revealed, it might indicate excessive borrowing or idle money that could be "put to work." The objective is to **finally** develop a plan which, if followed, will provide a well-managed flow of cash.

The Form: The cash flow projection form provides a systematic method of recording estimates of cash receipts and expenditures, which can be compared with actual receipts and expenditures as they become known—hence the two columns, Estimate and Actual. The entries listed on the form will not necessarily apply to every business, and some entries may not be included which would be pertinent to specific businesses. It is suggested, therefore, that the form be adapted to the particular business for which the projection is being made, with appropriate changes in the entries as may be required. Before the cash flow projection can be completed and pricing structure established, it is necessary to know or to estimate various important factors of the business, for example: What are the direct costs of the product or services **per unit?** What are the monthly or yearly costs of the operation? What is the sales price per unit of the product or service? Determine that the pricing structure provides this business with reasonable breakeven goals (including a reasonable net profit) when conservative sales goals are met. What are the available sources of cash, other than income from sales; for example, loans, equity capital, rent, or other sources?

Procedure: Most of the entries for the form are self-explanatory; however, the following suggestions are offered to simplify the procedure:

(A) Suggest even dollars be used rather than showing cents.

(B) If this is a new business, or an existing business undergoing significant changes or alterations, the cash flow part of the column marked "Pre-start-up Position" should be completed. (Fill in appropriate blanks only.) Costs involved here are, for example, rent, telephone, and utilities deposits before the business is actually open. Other items might be equipment purchases, alterations, the owner's cash injection, and cash from loans received before actual operations begin.

(C) Next fill in the pre-start-up position of the essential operating data (non-cash flow information), where applicable.

(D) Complete the form using the suggestions in the partial form below for each entry.

CHECKING

In order to insure that the figures are properly calculated and balanced, they must be checked. Several methods may be used, but the following four checks are suggested as a minimum:

CHECK #1: Item #1 (Beginning Cash on Hand—1st Month) plus Item #3 (Total Cash Receipts — Total Column) minus Item #6 (Total Cash Paid Out—Total Column) should be equal to Item #7 (Cash Position at End of 12th Month).

CHECK #2: Item A (Sales Volume—Total Column) plus Item B (Accounts Receivable—Pre-start-up Position) minus Item 2(a)(Cash Sales—Total Column) minus Item 2(b)(Accounts Receivable Collection—Total Column) minus Item C (Bad Debt—Total Column) should be equal to Item B (Accounts Receivable at End of 12th Month).

CHECK #3: The horizontal total of Item #6 (Total Cash Paid Out) is equal to the vertical total of all items under Item #5 (5(a) through 5(w)) in the total column at the right of the form.

CHECK #4: The horizontal total of Item #3 (Total Cash Receipts) is equal to the vertical total of all items under #2 (2(a) through 2(c)) in the total column at the right of the form.

ANALYZE the correlation between the cash flow and the projected profit during the period in question. The estimated profit is the **difference** between the estimated change in assets and the estimated change in liabilities before such things as any owner withdrawal, appreciation of assets, change in investments, etc. (The change may be positive or negative.) This can be obtained as follows:

The **change in assets** before owner's withdrawal, appreciation of assets, change in investments, etc., can be computed by adding the following:

(1) Item #7 (Cash Position—End of Last Month) minus Item #1 (Cash on Hand at the Beginning of the First Month).

(2) Item #5(t)(Capital Purchases—Total Column) minus Item F (depreciation—Total Column).

(3) Item B. (Accounts Receivable—End of 12th Month) minus Item B (Accounts Receivable—Pre-start-up Position).

(4) Item D. (Inventory on Hand—End of 12th Month) minus Item D (Inventory on Hand—Pre-start-up Position).

(5) Item #5 (w) (Owner's withdrawal—Total Column) or dividends, minus such things as an increase in investment.

(6) Item #5 (v) (Reserve and/or Escrow—Total Column).

The **change in liabilities** (before items noted in "change in assets") can be computed by adding the following:

(1) Item 2(c) (Loans—Total Column) minus 5(s) (Loan Principal Payment—Total Column).

(2) Item E (Accounts Payable—End of 12th Month) minus E (Accounts Payable—Pre-start-up Position).

ANALYSIS

A. The cash position at the end of each month should be adequate to meet the cash requirements for the following month. If too little cash, then additional cash will have to be injected or cash paid out must be reduced. If there is too much cash on hand, the money is not working for your business.

B. The cash flow projection, the profit and loss projection, the breakeven analysis, and good cost control information are tools which, if used properly, will be useful in making decisions that can increase profits to insure success.

C. The projection becomes more useful when the estimated information can be compared with actual information as it develops. It is important to follow through and complete the actual columns as the information becomes available. Utilize the cash flow projection to assist in setting new goals and planning operations for more profit.

Please Note: Public reporting burden for this collection of information is estimated to average 1 hour per response, including the time for reviewing instructions, searching existing data sources, gathering and maintaining the data needed, and completing and reviewing the collection of information. Send comments regarding this burden estimate or any other aspect of this collection of information, including suggestions for reducing this burden, to: Chief, Administrative Information Branch, William A. Cline, Room 200 U.S. Small Business Administration, 1441 L St., NW Washington, DC 20416; and to the Office of Information and Regulatory Affairs, Office of Management and Budget, Washington, DC 20503.

---

* Cash funds, for the purpose of this projection, are defined as cash, checks, or money order, paid out or received.

1. CASH ON HAND (Beginning of month)	Cash on hand same as (7), Cash Position Previous Month
2. CASH RECEIPTS	
(a) Cash Sales	All cash sales. Omit credit sales unless cash is actually received.
(b) Collections from Credit Accounts	Amount to be expected from all credit accounts.
(c) Loan or Other Cash Injection	Indicate here all cash injections not shown in 2(a) or 2(b) above. See "A" of "Analysis"
3. TOTAL CASH RECEIPTS (2a + 2b + 2c = 3)	Self-explanatory
4. TOTAL CASH AVAILABLE (Before cash out) (1 + 3)	Self-explanatory
5. CASH PAID OUT	
(a) Purchases (Merchandise)	Merchandise for resale or for use in product (paid for in current month)
(b) Gross Wages (Excludes withdrawals)	Base pay plus overtime (if any)
(c) Payroll Expenses (Taxes, etc.)	Include paid vacations, paid sick leave, health insurance, unemployment insurance, etc. (this might be 10 to 45% OF 5(b)
(d) Outside Services	This could include outside labor and/or material for specialized or overflow work, including subcontracting
(e) Supplies (Office and operating)	Items purchased for use in the business (not for resale)
(f) Repairs and Maintenance	Include periodic large expenditures such as painting or decorating
(g) Advertising	This amount should be adequate to maintain sales volume—include telephone book yellow page cost
(h) Car, Delivery, and Travel	If personal car is used, charge in this column—include parking
(i) Accounting and Legal	Outside services, including, for example, bookkeeping
(j) Rent	Real estate only (See 5(p) for other rentals)
(k) Telephone	Self-explanatory
(l) Utilities	Water, heat, light, and/or power
(m) Insurance	Coverages on business property and products e.g. fire, liability; also workman's compensation, fidelity, etc. Exclude "executive" life (include in "5W").
(n) Taxes (Real estate, etc.)	Plus inventory tax—sales tax—excise tax, if applicable
(o) Interest	Remember to add interest on loan as it is injected (See 2(c) above)
(p) Other Expenses (Specify each)	Unexpected expenditures may be included here as a safety factor
	Equipment expenses during the month should be included here (Non-capital equipment)
	When equipment is rented or leased, record payments here
(q) Miscellaneous (Unspecified)	Small expenditures for which separate accounts would not be practical
(r) Subtotal	This subtotal indicates cash out for operating costs
(s) Loan Principal Payment	Include payment on all loans, including vehicle and equipment purchases on time payment
(t) Capital Purchases (Specify)	Non-expensed (depreciable) expenditures such as equipment, building, vehicle purchases, and leasehold improvements
(u) Other Start-up Costs	Expenses incurred prior to first month projection and paid for after the "start-up" position
(v) Reserve and/or Escrow (Specify)	Example: insurance, tax, or equipment escrow to reduce impact of large periodic payments
(w) Owner's Withdrawal	Should include payment for such things as owner's income tax, social security, health insurance, "executive" life insurance premiums, etc.
6. TOTAL CASH PAID OUT (Total 5a thru 5w)	Self-explanatory
7. CASH POSITION (End of month) (4 minus 6)	Enter this amount in (1) Cash on Hand following month—See "A" of "Analysis"
ESSENTIAL OPERATING DATA (Non-cash flow information)	This is basic information necessary for proper planning and for proper cash flow-projection. In conjunction with this data, the cash flow can be evolved and shown in the above form.
A. Sales Volume (Dollars)	This is a very important figure and should be estimated carefully, taking into account size of facility and employee output as well as realistic anticipated sales (Actual sales performed—not orders received)
B. Accounts Receivable (End of month)	Previous unpaid credit sales plus current month's credit sales, less amounts received current month (deduct "C" below)
C. Bad Debt (End of month)	Bad debts should be subtracted from (B) in the month anticipated
D. Inventory on Hand (End of month)	Last month's inventory plus merchandise received and/or manufactured current month minus amount sold current month
E. Accounts Payable (End of month)	Previous month's payable plus current month's payable minus amount paid during month
F. Depreciation	Established by your accountant, or value of all your equipment divided by useful life (in months) as allowed by Internal Revenue Service

SBA FORM 1100 (1–83)

*U.S. Government Printing Office: 1989-269-864/00267

Cash flow

Cash Cycle. In any business, there is a continual cycle of events that can increase or decrease the cash balance. The following diagram is used to illustrate this flow of cash.

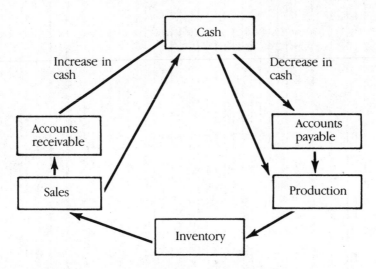

Cash is decreased in the acquisition of materials and services to produce the finished goods. It is reduced in paying off the amounts owed to suppliers: that is, accounts payable. Once this inventory is sold and cash is generated and accounts receivable, that is, money owed from customers. When customers pay, accounts receivable is reduced and the cash account increases. However, the cash flows are not necessarily related to the sales in that period because customers might pay in the next period.

Net working capital.   Current assets are those resources of cash and those assets that can be converted to cash within one year or a normal business cycle. These include cash, marketable securities, accounts receivable, inventories, etc. Current liabilities are obligations that become due within one year or a normal business cycle. These include accounts payable, notes payable, accrued expenses payable, etc. You might want to consider current assets as the source of funds that reduce current liabilities.

One way to measure the flow of cash and the firm's ability to maintain its cash or liquid assets is to compute *working capital*. Working capital is the difference between current assets and current liabilities. The change in this value from period to period is called *net working capital*. For example:

	19 × 1	19 × 2
Current assets	$110,000	$200,000
Less current liabilities	− 70,000	− 112,000
Working capital	40,000	88,000
Net Working capital Increase (Decrease)		$48,000

Net working capital increased during the year, but we don't know how. It could have been all in cash or all in inventory. Or, it might have resulted from a reduction in accounts payable.

Cash flow statement. While net working capital shows only the changes in the current position, a "flow" statement can be developed to explain the changes that have occurred in any account during any time period. The cash flow statement is an analysis of the cash inflows and outflows.

The ability to forecast cash requirements is indeed a means of becoming a more efficient manager. If you can determine the cash requirements for any period, you can establish a bank loan in advance, or you can reduce other current asset accounts so that the cash will be made available. Also, when you have excess cash, you can put this cash to productive use to earn a return.

The change in the cash account can be readily determined if you know net working capital and the changes in current liabilities and current assets other than cash.

Let:
NWC be net working capital
CA be the change in current
         assets other than cash
CL change in current liabilities
$cash$ be the change in cash

Because net working capital is the difference between the change in current assets and current liabilities,

$$NWC = CA + cash - CL$$
$$cash = NWC - CA + CL$$

This relationship states that, if we know net working capital (NWC), the change in current liabilities (CL), and the change in current assets less cash (CA less cash), we can calculate the change in cash. The change in cash is then added to the beginning balance of cash to determine the ending balance.

Suppose you forecast that sales will increase $50,000 and the following will correspondingly change:

Receivables	increase by $25,000
Inventory	increase by $70,000
Accounts payable	increase by $30,000
Notes payable	increase by $10,000

Using net working capital of $48,000, what is the projected change in cash?

$$cash = NWC - CA + CL$$
$$= 48,000 - 25,000 - 70,000 + 30,000 + 10,000$$
$$= -7,000$$

Over this time period, under the condition of increasing sales volume, cash decreases by $7,000. Is there enough cash to cover this decrease? This will depend on the beginning cash balance.

Sources and application of funds. At any given level of sales, it is easier to forecast the required inventory, accounts payable, receivables, etc., than net working capital. To forecast this net working capital account, you must trace the sources and application of funds. Sources of funds increase working capital. Applications of funds decrease working capital. The difference between the sources and applications of funds is the net working capital.

The following calculation is based on the fact that the balance sheet is indeed in "balance." That is, total assets equal total liabilities plus stockholders' equity.

$$\underset{\text{assets}}{\text{current}} + \underset{\text{assets}}{\text{noncurrent}} = \underset{\text{liabilities}}{\text{current}} + \underset{\text{liabilities}}{\text{long-term}} + \text{equity}$$

Rearranging this equation:

$$\underset{\text{assets}}{\text{current}} - \underset{\text{liabilities}}{\text{current}} - \underset{\text{liabilities}}{\text{long-term}} + \text{equity} - \underset{\text{assets}}{\text{noncurrent}}$$

Because the left-hand side of the equation is working capital, the right-hand side must also equal working capital. A change to either side is the net working capital. If long-term liabilities and equity increase or noncurrent assets decrease, net working capital increases. This change would be a source of funds. If noncurrent assets increase or long-term liabilities and equity decrease, net working capital decreases. This change would be an application of funds. Typical sources of funds or net working capital are:

- Funds provided by operations.
- Disposal of fixed assets.
- Issuance of stock.
- Borrowing from a long-term source.

To obtain the first source of funds, subtract all expense items requiring funds from all revenue that was a source of funds. You can also obtain this result in an easier manner: add back expenses that did not result in inflows or outflows of funds to reported net income.

The most common nonfund expense is depreciation, the allocation of the cost of an asset as an expense over the life of the asset against the future revenues produced. Adjusting net income with depreciation is much simpler than computing revenues and expenses that require funds. Again, depreciation is not a source of funds. The typical applications of funds or net working capital are:

- Purchase of fixed assets.
- Payment of dividends.
- Retirement of long-term liabilities.
- Repurchase of equity.

The following is an example of how sources and applications of funds might be used to determine net working capital.

Statement of sources and applications of funds

Sources of funds:
From operation

Net income	$10,000
Add back depreciation (noncash item)	15,000

	25,000
Issuance of debt	175,000
Issuance of stock	3,000
	$203,000
Application of funds:	
Purchase of plant	140,000
Cash dividends	15,000
	155,000
Net working capital increase (decrease)	$48,000

Statement of changes in financial position.   This statement combines two statements previously discussed: the statement of sources and application of funds and the changes in working capital accounts. This statement can be converted into a cash flow statement by solving for cash as the unknown, such as the following.

Cash flow statement

Sources of funds	$203,000
Applications of funds	155,000
Net working capital	$ 48,000
Less:	
Increase in receivables	25,000
Increase in inventory	70,000
	−95,000
	−47,000
Plus:	
Increase in accounts payable	30,000
Increase in notes payable	10,000
	40,000
Cash flow	$−7,000

Planning for cash flow

Cash flow can be used not only to determine how cash flowed through the business but also as an aid to determine the excess or shortage of cash. Suppose your analysis of cash flow forecasts a potential cash deficiency. You could then do a number of things, such as:

~ Increase borrowings: loans, stock issuance, etc.
~ Reduce current asset accounts: reduce receivables, inventory, etc.
~ Reduce noncurrent assets: postpone expanding the facility, sell off some fixed assets, etc.

By using a cash flow statement, you can determine if sufficient funds are available from financing activities, show funds generated from all sources, and show how these funds were applied. Using and adjusting the information gained from this cash flow analysis will help you to know in advance if there will be enough cash to pay:

• Supplier bills

- Interest
- Dividends

Careful planning will ensure a sufficient amount of cash to meet future obligations on schedule, which is essential for the "successful" business.

Planning aid

The following example is presented to help you develop a cash flow analysis. Of course, all names are fictitious. During the next month, Irene Smith, owner-manager of Imagine Manufacturing, expects sales to increase to $10,000. Based on past experience, she made this forecast:

Net income to be 9% of sales	$ 900
Income taxes to be 3.2% of sales	320
Accounts receivable to increase	5,000
Inventory to increase	2,000
Accounts payable to increase	3,000

Her beginning cash balance is $3,000 and she plans to purchase a piece of equipment for $1,500. What is her cash flow?

Cash flow analysis

Sources of funds:	
Net income	$ 900
Add back depreciation	1,000
	1,900
Application of funds:	
Addition to fixed assets	$1,500
Payment of taxes	320
	1,820
Net working capital increase (decrease)	$ 80
Working capital accounts:	
Less change in	
Inventory	$ − 2,000
Accounts receivable	− 5,000
Plus change in	
Accounts payable	3,000
Cash flow	$ − 3,920
Plus beginning cash balance	3,000
Equals ending cash balance	$ − 920

Assuming Irene's forecast is correct, she has a cash need of $920 next month. If she cannot borrow the additional funds, she must either reduce sales, which could reduce profits, or find another source of cash. She can now use her cash flow analysis to try to determine a source of funds or a reduction in the application of funds. An easy solution is to postpone the purchase of the equipment. This would increase her cash flow by $1,500, more than enough for a positive cash balance at the end of next month.

Pitfall 16

Letting your accountant run the business

The owner who made financial decisions without financial knowledge

"CHRIS, WHAT IS GOING ON WITH YOUR CHECKING ACCOUNT? ITS BEEN OVERDRAWN 15 out of the last 18 days. I can't keep covering these checks and you sure don't want to keep paying all the insufficient funds charges. If you can't get this thing covered by tomorrow, I'll have to start returning your checks unpaid."

Chris apologized to Tom, the bank vice president, and assured him he would have the problem cleared up immediately. He picked up the phone and called Ken, his accountant.

"Ken, I just had a nasty call from the bank about my checking account being overdrawn. I don't understand since the report you sent me at the beginning of the month had a very healthy balance. I've written some checks for rent and inventory, but not to the extent of that balance. Can you check it out for me?"

"Sure, Chris, but I bet I know what happened. Remember we discussed putting your loan payments and retirement fund contributions on an automatic deduction from your checking account basis? That started this month, and I'll bet you forgot. You add up all of the checks you have written and I'll add those amounts and see if that explains the problem."

Chris hung up furious. This was getting out of hand. He never knew how much money he had and was constantly getting surprises from his accountant. He had turned over all of his bookkeeping chores to Ken because he knew nothing about accounting. His only responsibility was to send the checkbook stubs and the deposit slips to Ken each month and Ken would do all the balancing, statements, and tax forms. Chris would receive a summary statement and Ken was to inform him of any unusual activity. Chris was careless in keeping track of suggestions such as the automatic account deductions and now he was in jeopardy of harming his good relationship with his bank.

Understanding basic bookkeeping

Chris has done what so many small business owners do—run away from accounting. There is a misperception that accounting requires an advanced degree in business to understand it. True, some tax reporting and financial statements are sometimes better left in the hands of an accountant, but the everyday bookkeeping chores should stay in the hands of the owner. Turning over all bookkeeping duties to an outside source is both expensive and dangerous.

The daily bookkeeping task of a small business become rather routine. It requires you to keep a daily sales journal, a disbursement journal, and a master ledger. All very simple to keep tabs on.

The daily sales journal is a record of receipts a business acquires. Moneys should be reconciled on a work sheet such as the one shown in Fig. 16–1 and then entered onto a sales journal (Fig. 16–2). The sales journal is totaled each month and gives a complete record of all revenue activity for that month. As you can see, it shows the sales, deposits, any discrepancies, refunds, and losses.

```
DAILY CASH RECONCILIATION

May 12, Monday (rainy and overcast)

Gross sales    $1407.60

Register readings    #1 687.90
                     #2 325.30
                     #3 394.40


Cash       $897.00
Coin          4.67
Checks      345.90
Visa         67.80
Master ch    54.85
           ------
Total      1370.30

overings     12.60
refunds      17.40
paid outs     6.50( postage)
           ------
Total      1406.80

Shortage       .80

Number of transactions   235
```

Fig. 16–1. Daily cash reconciliation.

SALES AND CASH RECEIPTS

FACSIMILE PAGE
ILLUSTRATING THE USE OF THIS
IDEAL SYSTEM FORM.

DISTRIBUTION OF SALES
(REPLACES FORMS 41, 131, 141)

THE IDEAL SYSTEM, REG. U S. PAT OFFICE MADE IN U S A

WHEN MERCHANDISE THAT HAS PREVIOUSLY BEEN ENTERED IN THIS SECTION IS RETURNED TO YOU FOR CREDIT -- ENTER AND CIRCLE THE AMOUNT (OR ENTER IN RED) - AND DEDUCT THE AMOUNT FROM THE COLUMNS CONCERNED.

COLUMNS WITH BLANK HEADINGS MAY BE USED TO KEEP TRACK OF ANY PARTICULAR CLASS OF SALES YOU WISH. FOR EXAMPLE: REPAIR DEPT.; APPLIANCE SALES; RETAIL SALES; WHOLESALE; LABOR; MATERIAL SALES; ETC; ETC.

THE MONTHLY TOTAL OF COLUMN 4 (TOTAL SALES) IS TO BE CARRIED ON LINE 1 (UNDER THE PROPER MONTH) ON THE SUMMARY OF BUSINESS AND STATEMENT OF INCOME FORMS.

YOU MAY EITHER SUMMARIZE THE ENTIRE DAYS SALES, AND CASH RECEIPTS ON ONE LINE EACH DAY - IN WHICH CASE YOUR ENTIRE MONTHS ENTRIES WILL BE ON ONE PAGE - OR YOU MAY USE AS MANY LINES DAILY AND AS MANY PAGES MONTHLY AS ARE NEEDED TO ITEMIZE EACH TRANSACTION EACH DAY.

TRANSFER ALL OF THE MONTHLY TOTALS TO FORM 5-21 SUMMARY (LAST PAGE OF THIS SECTION). THIS GIVES YOU A MONTH BY MONTH COMPARISON OF YOUR SALES - IN EACH DEPARTMENT OF YOUR BUSINESS - SHOWING YOU EXACTLY HOW YOUR BUSINESS IS PROGRESSING.

Fig. 16–2. Sales and cash journal.

FACSIMILE PAGE
ILLUSTRATING THE USE OF THIS IDEAL SYSTEM FORM 23.

PAYMENTS — ALL CASH AND CHECKS PAID OUT

IDEAL SYSTEM - FORM 23

THE IDEAL SYSTEM, REG. U. S. PAT. OFFICE. MADE IN U. S. A.

THE IDEAL SYSTEM · REG. U. S. PAT. OFFICE

BANK DEPOSITS	BANK BALANCE (2+1−3)	DATE 19—	CHECK NUMBER	TO WHOM PAID	MEMORANDA	PAID OUT BY CHECK	PAID OUT BY CASH	DEDUCTIONS FROM EMPLOYEE'S EARNINGS — F O A B & WITHHOLD (4A)	UNEMP INS (4B)	OTHER INCT AL DEDUCTIONS (4C)	CASH DISCOUNT TAKEN	MERCHANDISE

ENTER THE DETAILS OF EACH EMPLOYEES EARNINGS AND DEDUCTIONS ON THE EMPLOYEE'S INDIVIDUAL COMPENSATION RECORD (FORM G-B12) IN THE BACK OF THIS BOOK, THUS SIMPLIFYING THE PREPARATION OF YOUR VARIOUS PAYROLL TAX RETURNS.

YOU MAY USE AS MANY LINES DAILY AND AS MANY PAGES MONTHLY AS ARE NEEDED TO ENTER ALL PAYMENTS

ACCOUNTS FOR ALL CHECKS AND FOR ALL CASH PAID OUT.

USE TWO LINES WHEN NECESSARY.

AT THE END OF EACH MONTH — — ENTER THE ENTIRE MONTHS TOTALS OF EACH COLUMN ON THE LAST LINE — AND ALSO ENTER UNDER THE PROPER MONTH ON FORMS S-23R+B (LAST PAGES IN THIS SECTION) AND ON FORMS 24A,B +C SUMMARY OF BUSINESS AND STATEMENT OF INCOME.

TOTALS

Fig. 16–3. Disbursement journal.

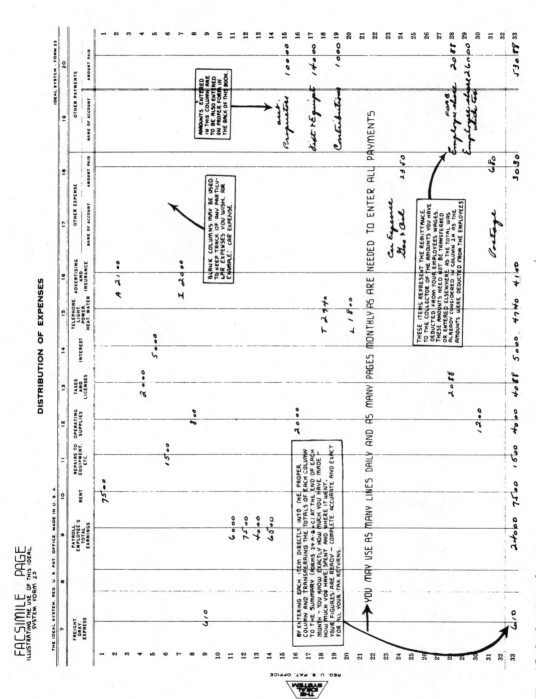

Fig. 16–3. Continued.

FACSIMILE PAGE
ILLUSTRATING THE USE OF THIS IDEAL SYSTEM FORM 23

DISTRIBUTION OF EXPENSES

THE IDEAL SYSTEM. REG. U. S. PAT. OFFICE. MADE IN U. S. A. — IDEAL SYSTEM · FORM 23

	7	8	9	10	11	12	13	14	15	16	17	18	19	20	
	FREIGHT. DRAY. EXPRESS		PAYROLL. EMPLOYEE'S TOTAL EARNINGS	RENT	REPAIRS TO EQUIPMENT. ETC.	OPERATING SUPPLIES	TAXES AND LICENSES	INTEREST	TELEPHONE. LIGHT. POWER. HEAT. WATER	ADVERTISING AND INSURANCE	OTHER EXPENSE: NAME OF ACCOUNT	OTHER EXPENSE: AMOUNT PAID	OTHER PAYMENTS: NAME OF ACCOUNT	OTHER PAYMENTS: AMOUNT PAID	
1				75 00											1
2										A 21 00					2
3															3
4							20 00								4
5								50 00							5
6					15 00										6
7										I 20 00					7
8						8 00									8
9	6 10														9
10															10
11			60 00												11
12			75 00												12
13			40 00												13
14			65 00												14
15													acct. Proprietor	100 00	15
16						20 00									16
17													Lift & Equipt	140 00	17
18									T 29 40						18
19													Contributions	10 00	19
20									L 18 00						20
21															21
22															22
23											Car Expense				23
24											Gas & Oil	23 50			24
25															25
26															26
27															27
28							20 88						FOAB Employee share	20 88	28
29													Employee share withh. tax	260 00	29
30						12 00									30
31											Postage	6 80			31
32															32
33	6 10		240 00	75 00	15 00	40 00	40 88	50 00	47 40	41 00		30 30		530 88	33

BY ENTERING EACH ITEM DIRECTLY INTO THE PROPER COLUMN AND TRANSFERRING THE TOTALS OF EACH COLUMN TO THE SUMMARY (FORMS 24 A-B-C) AT THE END OF EACH MONTH ~ YOU KNOW EXACTLY HOW MUCH YOU HAVE MADE ~ HOW MUCH YOU HAVE SPENT AND WHERE IT WENT. YOUR FIGURES ARE READY ~ COMPLETE. ACCURATE AND EXACT FOR ALL YOUR TAX RETURNS.

→ YOU MAY USE AS MANY LINES DAILY AND AS MANY PAGES MONTHLY AS ARE NEEDED TO ENTER ALL PAYMENTS

BLANK COLUMNS MAY BE USED TO KEEP TRACK OF ANY PARTICULAR EXPENSES YOU WISH. FOR EXAMPLE: CAR EXPENSE.

AMOUNTS ENTERED IN THIS COLUMN ARE TO BE ALSO ENTERED ON PROPER FORM IN THE BACK OF THIS BOOK.

THESE ITEMS REPRESENT THE REMITTANCE TO THE COLLECTOR OF THE AMOUNTS YOU HAVE DEDUCTED FROM YOUR EMPLOYEES WAGES. THESE AMOUNTS NEED NOT BE TRANSFERRED OR ENTERED ELSEWHERE AS THE TOTAL WAS ALREADY CONSIDERED IN COLUMN 2A AS THE AMOUNTS WERE DEDUCTED FROM THE EMPLOYEES

THE IDEAL SYSTEM — REG. U. S. PAT. OFFICE

Fig. 16–3. Continued.

The disbursement journal uses the same procedure you follow in your personal checking account except that it requires you to break down your payouts into their proper classifications (see Fig. 16–3). By totaling all columns, you receive a complete picture of all expenditures for a month.

Recordkeeping

At this point, you can fill out a rough income statement for the month or if you want, your accountant can put this together for you (see Fig. 16–4). Just by doing these

```
                     INCOME STATEMENT
            FOR THE YEAR ENDING DECEMBER 31, 19XX
```

	ACTUAL $	% of SALES
SALES		
Greeting cards	$160,000	80.0%
Gifts	40,000	20.0
Total Sales	200,000	100.0
COST OF GOODS SOLD		
Cost of Sales	100,000	50.0
Freight	4,000	2.0
Discounts on merchandise	(1,000)	(1.0)
Mark downs, empl. disc.	5,000	2.5
Shrinkage	6,000	3.0
Total cost of goods sold	114,000	57.0
GROSS PROFIT	86,000	43.0
OPERATING EXPENSES		
Payroll	31,000	15.5
Rent	20,000	10.0
Maintenance & Repairs	1,600	0.8
Operating supplies	4,200	2.1
Taxes & Licenses	2,000	1.0
Utilities	3,800	1.9
Advertising	3,000	1.5
Insurance	2,400	1.2
Accounting & Legal	2,000	1.0
Miscellaneous	3,000	1.5
Total Cash Operating Expenses	73,000	36.5
Depreciation	5,000	2.5
Interest	6,000	3.0
Total Operating Expenses	84,000	42.0
PRE-TAX PROFIT	$2,000	1.0%

Fig. 16–4. Balance sheet.

two simple functions, you have eliminated the need for a bookkeeping service on a daily basis and have assured yourself that you know the financial status of the business.

The general or master ledger is a record of all the assets and liabilities of your business. In its summarized form, it makes up the balance sheet or statement of condition. It requires the recording of any assets purchased by the business and any liabilities, or debts, incurred by the business. Its purpose is to tell you how much you own as opposed to how much you owe. The asset sheets have individual sheets for each classification of assets, i.e., furniture, machinery, inventory, cash. The liability sheets have individual sheets for each classification of liabilities, i.e. accounts payable, notes payable, taxes payable. Each time a capital or liability account is paid on it, it must be recorded in the general ledger. This allows you to put together a balance sheet that shows the net value of the business whenever you need it.

Many businesses, particularly those without the use of a computer, allow their accountants to handle the master ledger. If you have the use of a small computer, it can be of great assistance in your bookkeeping functions. The most important advice on setting up a computer system is to find the software best suited for your needs first, then buy the computer that compliments that software best. Because small

Pay period ending 01-10-85

	Hours	Base Salary	Comm'n	Makeup	Total Salary		Bonus	Total Pay	FICA	W/H	Store Charge	Insur	Total Deduc	Net
	Kitchen Hours	Kitchen Salary	Waitrs Hours	Waitrs Salary	Total Salary	Tips	Bonus	Total Pay	FICA	W/H	Store Charge	Insur	Total Deduc	Net
Women's	152.75	639.63	0.00	0.00	639.63	0.00	0.00	639.63	45.09	49.13	63.00	0.00	157.22	482.41
Restaurant	230.50	833.83	69.50	145.10	978.93	87.73	0.00	1066.66	75.20	73.47	20.00	16.43	185.10	793.83
Cards & Gifts	185.25	711.12	0.00	0.00	711.12	0.00	0.00	711.12	50.13	41.78	0.00	0.00	91.91	619.21
Management	0.00	0.00	0.00	0.00	923.07	0.00	0.00	923.07	65.08	133.96	0.00	0.00	199.04	724.03
Clerical	44.25	199.13	0.00	0.00	199.13	0.00	0.00	199.13	14.04	18.23	0.00	0.00	32.27	166.86
Totals	612.75	2383.71	69.50	145.10	3451.88	87.73	0.00	3539.61	249.54	316.57	83.00	16.43	665.54	2786.34

Fig. 16–5. Payroll computer report.

businesses are so varied, it is difficult to find a system that exactly matches your needs, therefore, some functions will have to be performed manually. You will find, however, that all businesses can utilize a PC computer in the following three areas:

1. Payroll. If you run a payroll for more than three employees, a payroll program can save you many hours by calculating withholding taxes, F.I.C.A. taxes, doing W-2 forms, etc. It will also allow you to have a valuable summary of where your payroll expenses are going to as shown in Fig. 16–5.

2. Financial statements. The computer will print out your income statement for any period once you have entered the information from the sales and dis-

```
                   BALANCE SHEET
                 DECEMBER 31, 19XX

                       ASSETS
CURRENT ASSETS
   Cash                                  $28,000
   Inventory                              47,500
   Other Current Assets                    1,000
      Total Current Assets                76,500

FIXED ASSETS                              30,000

TOTAL ASSETS                             106,500

        LIABILITIES AND OWNER'S EQUITY

CURRENT LIABILITIES

Accounts Payable                          27,000
Current Portion - long term debt          10,000
   Total Current Liabilities              37,000

LONG TERM DEBT                            40,000

TOTAL LIABILITIES                         77,000

OWNER'S EQUITY                            29,500

TOTAL LIABILITIES & OWNER'S EQUITY      $106,500
```

Fig. 16–6. Income statement.

bursement journals. It is also easy to format a trial balance sheet once you enter the figures from the general ledger. (See Fig. 16–6.)

3. Accounts payable and accounts receivable. A simple entering of any invoices received or billed will enable you to have an up-to-date picture printed out of where you stand in regard to your creditors and those you extend credit to. This program will show you what is current or what is 30, 60, 90, or more days overdue.

There are many other functions, such as inventory control, that computers might or might not be able to assist you with. The cost of computers has come down to the point where they are affordable to any business that can make proper use of them.

Pitfall #16 summary
Bookkeeping checklist

Your bookkeeping system should include the following records. You can find these systems at your local office supply store.

1. Cash receipts—used to record all income received.

2. Cash disbursements—used to record all expenses paid.

3. Purchases—used to record all purchases and for maintaining inventories.

4. Payroll—a record for each employee and a summary of all payroll expenses.

5. Income statement and balance sheet—provides a month-by-month status on how your business is progressing.

6. Bank account—provides a monthy bank statement and reconciliation.

7. Depreciation schedule—shows a monthly calculation of depreciation on either a straight line or accelerated basis.

8. Accounts receivable and accounts payable—Provides a list of accounts and a record of all account transactions.

9. Supporting schedules—ledger sheets to record bad debts, insurance requests, notes payable, and plant and equipment acquisitions.

Pitfall 17

Ineffective inventory planning

Too many suppliers, too many headaches

"TOM, CAN YOU HELP ME? I HAVE GOT A TREMENDOUS MESS OF PAPERWORK. I SPEND my whole day stuck back here in my office and hardly anytime out on the sales floor. I can't keep up with all the invoices and checking in and recording all the new arrivals." Debbie was truly frustrated.

Tom was a retail consultant with many years of retail experience. It wasn't hard for him to identify the problem with a quick look around the tremendously over-crowded novelty gift and card shop. The store, The Potpourri Card and Gift Shop, was truly a hodgepodge of merchandise assortment. It was 1,500 square feet of gifts and paper products with little coordination of theme. It was a rather trashy presentation of hundreds of products displayed on tables, free-standing racks, and wall shelving.

"Debbie how many different companies do you buy from? What do you consider your major classifications?"

"Gee, Tom, I have no idea. Probably at least 50 or 60 suppliers, and I really have not given thought to classifications."

Tom pulled out a blank inventory tablet and handed it to Debbie. "Let's start by listing all of the companies you have bought from in the past year and the type of product. Then go back and check your sales reports to see what percentage each type of product is to your total store volume. We need to arrive at a plan of controlling your buying procedures." The completed list looked as follows:

Classification	# of suppliers	% of sales
greeting cards	5	19
other paper products	9	12
novelty gifts–under $10	14	27

novelty gifts–over $10	7	11
occasion gifts–under $10	9	12
occasion gifts–over $10	6	11
fine gifts–over $25	4	8
totals	54	100

"Debbie, it is not feasible to operate your store with an average sales per supplier of less than 2 percent.(100% / 54). You need to consolidate your suppliers and concentrate on where you are getting the highest return per classification. If you were able to raise your sales per supplier to 5 percent, you would save considerably on administrative time, not to say anything about the tremendous savings on freight bills. You might possibly receive some quantity discounts and better treatment from your suppliers. Let's pare down this list to something more manageable."

After further evaluation and review of supplier results, the list looked like this:

classification	# of suppliers	% to sales
greeting cards	3	19
other paper products	3	12
novelty gifts–under $10	5	27
novelty gifts–over $10	3	11
occasion gifts–under $10	3	12
occasion gifts–over $10	3	11
fine gifts–over $25	2	8
totals	22	100

"You should find that, by careful selection of these suppliers, you will be able to offer just as fine of a selection as you are currently offering. Those vendors that do not perform up to your expectations must be eliminated in order to add ones that will. It is a revolving cycle that must be kept on top of at all times. Small stores must make the best use of cooperative and dependable suppliers. You do not have the staff or the resources to operate under a buy at will philosophy. The buying plan is the most important ingredient to expense control. The idea is to maximize sales on a minimum investment."

Planning for maximum profits

Effective inventory planning is not only having the right goods at the right place, but also at the right time and at the right investment. Because the small business depends on the absolute control of all expenses to ensure a profit, it must be vitally concerned with what is normally the largest outflow of money—the cost of goods. If a business can cut its cost of goods by 2 percent, it is 2 percent of sales that will show up directly in the profit column. On a $300,000 volume business, that would be $6,000 that can go to the owner just by keeping on top of a good plan.

Inventory is the number of units and the value attached to those units that is available for sale or manufacture in the normal course of business. The goal is to find how many units are needed to reach a sales objective that produces the maximum amount of profit possible with the least amount of dollars invested. It is not an exact science and will never be performed to perfection, because it depends on market conditions, however, with astute planning and experience, it can be controlled to a point of assuring a profitable level.

Creating a purchase plan

Cost of sales cannot be figured just by referring to the amount of inventory purchases without accounting for changes in inventory position and the amount of discounts and losses the business sustains. The formula used is:

- beginning inventory
- plus purchases
- plus freight
- minus ending inventory
- equals cost of sales

The secret to the accuracy of this cost of sales is taking a proper ending inventory at its proper value. This evaluation of inventory will account for all discounts, or markdowns, and losses from theft or damage. In other words, the difference between the total value of what you have and what you should have had after deducting sales that has been stolen or discounted at cost.

To arrive at a proper buying plan, you must first start with setting your objective in regards to what you want to have for an ending inventory value before deciding on your purchase budget. Because the ending inventory is partially determined by losses and discounts, you will need to subtract the average percent of those expected during the time frame for which you are buying.

For example, a store wants to increase its inventory 10 percent during a six-month buying period. If its starting inventory is $50,000, the goal is to have an inventory of $55,000 after all purchases, sales, and discounts or losses have occurred. The plan used is as follows:

Beginning inventory	$ 50,000
Plus purchases	159,000
Minus sales	(140,000)
Minus discounts, losses (10%)	(14,000)
Ending inventory	$ 55,000

Making sure all figures are using the same valuation, in this case, retail value, this store must purchase $159,000 worth of merchandise to assure enough inventory is on hand to reach its sales objective of $140,000.

Therefore, a buying plan can be created after the buyer declares an ending inventory objective, a sales projection, and an adjustment for markdowns and losses incurred. It covers a certain period of time, and then for budgetary reasons, is broken into shorter time intervals. Figure 17–1 shows the previous buying plan broken down into a monthly buying budget.

Pitfall #17 summary
A sample purchase plan

Use this blank purchase planning form for a trial run. Start by writing in the beginning inventory figure and the anticipated ending inventory figure for the end of the period. Enter the projected sales for each month. Add the purchases necessary to achieve sales, and remember to subtract out planned markdowns for the month.

	JULY	AUG.	SEPT.	OCT.	NOV.	DEC.	TOTAL
BEG INVEN-TORY							
+ PUR-CHASES							
(-) SALES							
(-) MARK-DOWNS							
= END INVEN-TORY							

Fig. 17–1. Purchasing plan.

Pitfall 18

Chaotic management

The enterpreneur who couldn't make the transition from the corporate world

JOE MORRISON WAS WELL SCHOOLED IN MANAGEMENT PRACTICES. HE HAD A DEGREE in business and had spent eight years as a supervisor for a large sporting goods company. He knew how to schedule, collect information, evaluate personnel, and conduct market research studies. When David Cagle asked him to join him in the purchase of a wholesale sports equipment business, he didn't hesitate.

Joe and David's friendship went back 10 years. David was the creative and impulsive one, while Joe was the well organized, detail-oriented one. It seemed that they would complement each other's strengths and weaknesses. David was president in charge of marketing and Joe was the vice president in charge of daily operations. David traveled to trade shows to sell and meet with sales representative to buy, while Joe handled all of the operations, including shipping, personnel, and administrative duties.

Problems started immediately as Joe was confronted with the tremendous amount of duties required to keep a staff of nine producing at acceptable levels.

He would start each day by reviewing the incoming orders and posting them to the daily shipping schedule. David was doing an excellent job of selling, making shipping a real challenge. Joe worked at great detail on a scheduling and order-filling plan that would assure on-time delivery. He used a plan that he had developed in his old position and had always proved successful. He used elaborate charts and computer printouts to explain the system to the employees. These tools required daily updating, which absorbed a tremendous amount of his time. The key to success was maximum output from each worker.

Unfortunately, the plan did not allow for absenteeism. Often, one or more employees would call in sick on a given day, which would force Joe to drop his other duties in order to fill in. This conflicted with his orderly plan and proved very frustrating. In his previous job, he had always been able to call personnel to send a replacement worker to fill in for an absent person. That wasn't possible in a small company.

Joe was also frustrated with the degree of incompetence of the workers. The difficulty of recruiting skilled labor on a small company budget often resulted in hiring less capable people than he was used to. Consequently, a lot of time was spent repeatedly reviewing procedures and techniques as he trained personnel.

He also wished for more communication with David. David's traveling schedule made regular management and staff meetings impossible. They were held on a hit and miss basis. He was used to regular weekly meetings in the old corporation.

The problems came to a head six months into the job. David was greeted on return from a sales trip with a request for a confidential meeting by key employees that did not include Joe.

"David, Joe is driving us crazy," Clara stated from the head of the table. "He has absolutely no patience or tolerance with us. He is obsessed with meeting deadlines and is always on our case. We are doing our best but it is never good enough. When he has to fill in he is so angry it upsets all of us. I personally don't know why he gets so annoyed. The only thing it interrupts is his time making all those stupid charts he is always showing us that make no sense. Tell him to back off or there will be some resignations real soon."

The meeting continued along the same lines. Each employee suggesting the same complaint. Joe was showing no flexibility in his approach to problems and couldn't handle any change in his routine.

The timing of this couldn't have been worse for David. He had returned to discuss an opportunity with Joe concerning purchasing a newly bankrupt company's inventory at a great price. The inventory would add a new product line that would complement their existing offerings. He decided to postpone the employee problem until he had a chance to get Sam's okay on the purchase because the decision had to be made within 72 hours or the bank that had foreclosed would sell the merchandise to an out of state business.

There was to be no putting off, however. Joe's reaction to David's proposal was, "No way David, we can't do that without a complete market research and analysis report. It will take two months to put that together." David immediately turned on Joe in a tirade about his inflexibility in all matters, including employees, and reminded him emphatically that he no longer worked for a large corporation and that the procedures were different in a small business.

The importance of proper delegation

Joe experienced what many who make the transition from the corporate or large organizational environment to the small business environment do. Gone are the supporting cast members. Small businesses are operated with a core of personnel, all directly involved with the mission at hand. Seldom will you find staff positions such as a personnel manager or marketing research analyst in small companies. Gone also are the numerous committees that are part of large organizations. In there place is a lean machine of determination waging combat with far less arsenal than the big boys. Budget restraints keep the organization streamlined. Management in this arena is more challenging and can only be successful if kept flexible.

Joe was not flexible, nor could he adapt quickly enough to make decisions. His former organizations structure protected him from the internal mechanics of getting on with the job. The other problem that was haunting him was the inability to properly delegate. In a small business, everyone wears many hats. You can't possibly do it all. It is imperative to devise a delegation system that assures completion of assignments. This requires effective training, but must be built into the system. The recruiting of personnel on a limited budget often hampers the skill level of employees, therefore, effective training is mandatory.

Management functions

Basic management principles are valid in all businesses, regardless of size. A good manager plans, organizes, directs, staffs, and controls. Unfortunately, as Joe learned, a small business manager often also works in operations.

Planning means preparing for the future. Too many entrepreneurs are so involved with the day-to-day activities of the business that they don't take the time to consider where they must be six months, a year, or five years down the road. Proper selling, buying, financing, advertising and staffing must have sufficient lead time if they are to be effective. A good manager builds time into each day for contemplating the future direction and goals of the company.

Organizing requires assigning tasks. This delegation process must be well thought out. Charting personnel strengths and weaknesses is a good tool to use in deciding whom to assign what tasks.

Directing is the everyday overseeing of operations. Ensuring that instructions are followed and procedures are adhered to. In a small business, this translates into making sure the team is working effectively toward the goals of the business. It requires patience, tolerance, and the willingness to pitch in when necessary.

Staffing is making sure there is sufficient and capable personnel on hand to do the job. Just as in large companies, small businesses should use management tools such as job descriptions and organization charts (see Figs. 18–1 and 18–2). Job descriptions are more general in small businesses and responsibilities overlap, but they are still necessary to ensure that employees knows what their responsibilities are. The organization chart might be small, but it is necessary to show employees where they fit into the company.

Controlling is the tool used to check performance against standards. Large companies often use formal evaluation forms. A small company doesn't need to be as formal, but it must still communicate with employees how their work stacks up to standards. It is only fair to the employees to allow feedback on how their performance is judged. It should be done in an informal method over coffee, lunch, or an after-hours beer. It is not necessary to be stuffy about it, but it is necessary that it be

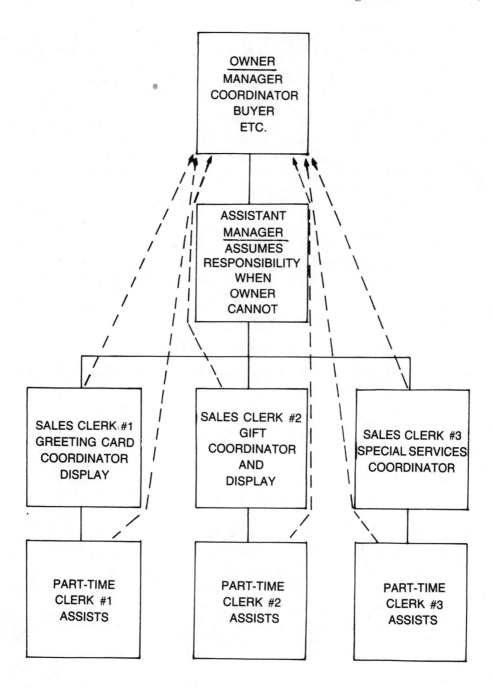

Fig. 18–1. Organization chart.

**Job Description
Sales Clerk #2**

Primary responsibilities: Assist customers in the selection and purchase of merchandise. Exemplify courteous manner at all times. Coordinate placement of gift merchandise on shelves in attractive display. Oversee pricing and unpacking of gift merchandise. Arrange for creative display of merchandise, including necessary signing and accent pieces.

Secondary responsibilities: Assist fellow employees in completing their responsibilities. Keep informed of all store policies and procedures. Become knowledgeable of features, advantages, and selling points of all store merchandise. Complete all housekeeping chores assigned.

Fig. 18–2. Job description.

done and recorded in some manner. Good management is good communication with employees. The key to successful small business management is simplicity and honesty.

Pitfall #18 summary
A manager profile

A manager wears many hats. The silhouette below shows the many roles you will play as the manager of a small business.

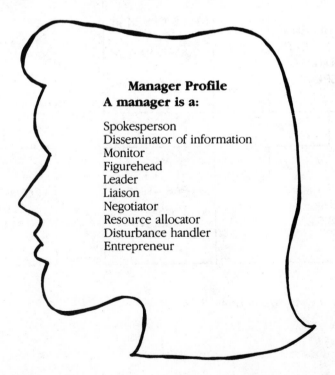

**Manager Profile
A manager is a:**

Spokesperson
Disseminator of information
Monitor
Figurehead
Leader
Liaison
Negotiator
Resource allocator
Disturbance handler
Entrepreneur

Pitfall 19

Expanding for the wrong reasons

The owner who got too big for his britches.

"MARGARET, WE ARE REALLY DOING WELL. I PAID ALL OF THE CHRISTMAS INVOICES TO-day and there is still over $15,000 in the checking account. We should consider opening another store in Lake Plaza. I certainly think I could handle two stores. It would be fun. Anyhow, I'm bored with just one store."

"Larry, you are forgetting we still owe $30,000 to the bank on this store. I don't think we should do anything until after that is paid," Margaret cautioned.

"C'mon Margaret, those monthly payments are easy. I'll bet they would loan us the money on a new store based on how prompt our payments have been. I'm going down and talk to the bank and see what they say."

Larry was right. His banking friend, Keith, was favorable. The bank looked upon Larry as an up and coming young businessman that would do quite well and were anxious to accommodate his request. Three months later, Larry had his new store. It was exciting and gratifying. The stores carried Larry's name, Jacob's Store for Men, and were gaining recognition throughout the county as the leading fashion store for men. Larry enjoyed the recognition he received throughout the area.

This started a pattern of growth that was quite phenomenal. The excitement Larry felt each time he opened or enlarged a store was his motivation. He expanded his original store to double its size, opened a third store in the third community in the county, and then reached into the neighboring county and opened two stores. All this occurred in a two-year period.

He was so busy and excited he didn't notice that he was missing the mark on some of his outlets. The new outlets were adding to his cash flow, but not neces-sarily to his profits. His accountant cautioned him to slow down, as did his wife, who were becoming concerned about the growing debt each time he opened a store.

145

Meanwhile, Larry was enjoying the notoriety. Shopping center developers were calling him every time a new center would open, his suppliers were treating him with great respect, and the communities were proud to have his stores. The bank was more than pleased with his growing deposits. He was at the peak of his short career and it was fun. He didn't want it to stop.

Larry was into a pattern that, when he felt a financial pinch, he would use his good reputation to borrow more money from the bank to open a new store. If he needed $40,000 to open a store, he would borrow $50,000 to cover some of his past due accounts. He kept this pattern up for five years and built a network of seven stores. It worked until the economy hit a recession. Interest rates went up as sales went down. Larry found himself in serious trouble with the bank and his suppliers. The problems escalated until he was forced into bankruptcy. The world came tumbling down on this once happy and carefree entrepreneur. How he wished he had heeded Margaret's advice years ago to payoff before moving ahead. His ego had gotten in the way of sound decisions.

Determining the right time to expand

Expanding your business is exciting. So exciting it might cloud your vision as to what is logical. Larry's immaturity lead him into disaster. He never properly planned his future. His decisions were made by intuition, not by rational and objective measures. What was very possibly a good opportunity was squandered because of ego, restlessness, and ambition. Once involved, he was trapped into a situation he could not get out of. Expanding your business is necessary to keep up with the market, but it must be done in consideration of timing, debt, and demand, not just personal desires.

Proper expansion is executed by following the same procedures as opening a new business. It is researched by collecting information on the market and follows a business plan.

The starting place is the profit and loss statement. You are looking for the point in time when it is necessary to expand to gain profits. A business' size can limit it as to a point of profit saturation. When it is established that profits cannot rise past a certain point without the addition of space, product line, or additional outlets, it is time to move forward. For example, if a business that has been moving forward at a certain acceptable rate of growth over a period of time suddenly stops losing its momentum it needs to evaluate a few factors. If there has been no change in market conditions or a drop in reinvestment of profits, there is reason to consider expansion. This is called the strategic window.

The strategic window refers to that period of time when all indicators for expansion are favorable. Profits are good, competition is weakened, the economy is strong, and future demand looks promising. On a business growth chart such as the one shown in Fig. 19–1, it usually is that period of time at the upper limit of the growth phase. This usually happens after the company passes through a strong introductory period that has carried over into a strong growth situation. If not acted, upon, the business will pass into the maturity stage and eventually will head for decline.

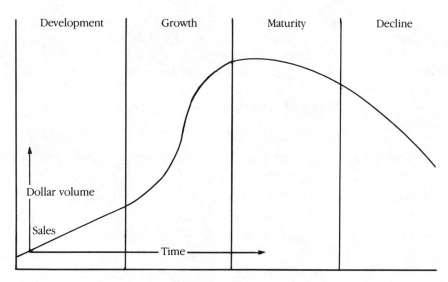

Fig. 19–1. Business growth chart.

It is important to point out that, depending on the owner's personal situation, such as age and ambition, it might be desirable to pass into the maturity stage—the stage where the owner is quite content to preserve the status quo if it agrees with her goals.

The decision of whether or not to expand is not limited to major changes. Expansion might be as simple as adding a new product line to a retail store. It might be accomplished by adding additional shelving or fixturing to your business. Often, an expansion goal can be reached by better using the assets on hand as opposed to an outlay of capital in order for a complete makeover or location change. Converting storage space to selling or production space is an example of expanding without spending.

Expansion planning

It takes cash and profits to finance an expansion, and the return on investment will not come overnight. Just as a new business, it will take time to recover the investment. Time costs money. If extra capital is not available to finance the expansion, it will have to be put off until the next strategic window opens. Before deciding whether or not to expand, ask yourself the following questions:

- Does the market have the necessary growth potential?
- What is the competition doing?
- Will the value added to the business produce the additional capital needed to pay back the investment in a reasonable period of time?
- Are there new markets to be served?
- Has anything happened to change the marketplace?

If you feel the answer to these questions will be positive, verify them. Go back to step one of your business plan. Study the demographics, do a new market analysis, a new cash flow projection, check with industry sources, and make sure that what you are planning fits your personal and financial goals.

Pitfall #19 summary
Expansion questionnaire

Before planning for an expansion, put your proposed idea to the following test. Be prepared to defend any negative answers.

1. Has the business revenues increased for each of the past three years?

2. Has the business net profits increased during each of the past three years?

3. Was the past year's sales and profit increase percentage down slightly from the previous two years? Is this due to space limitations?

4. Have you attempted all internal methods of expanding that do not require large capital outlays?

5. Have you written a business plan for your proposed expansion?

6. Have you researched your market to determine whether it is in a growth cycle?

7. Have you made a close inspection of how well your competition is doing? Do you foresee new competition coming into the marketplace?

8. Do you have a plan that accounts for hiring needed personnel to handle the additional activity?

9. Have you reviewed your plan with all lenders or investors that participate in your business?

10. Are your vendors able to supply you with all of the needed equipment and inventory necessary to assure your success.

11. Do you have the support of your family and employees for your proposed expansion?

12. Are you psychologically and physically prepared to handle the increased responsibilities and duties the expansion will require?

Pitfall 20

Believing that you will work forever

The business owner who waited too long to retire

JOE CABRELLA READ THE LETTER FROM CAMERON, INC. A THIRD TIME IN DISBELIEF. Cameron was switching to another supplier for their loading equipment. It was the third shock in the last three months. His largest customer for his company's parcel carrier was on an indefinite strike and not ordering, his second largest had decided to make the equipment in house, and now Cameron was lost to the competition. That left Joe with only one major account, an aerospace company whose needs were determined by erratic defense contracts. Basically, he was left with a 4,000 square foot, thoroughly equipped, manufacturing plant and very little to produce. After building the business for 20 years, he was faced with possible extinction. Joe was 67-years-old.

He thought about past decisions. Over the years he had built a successful operation. Starting with small accounts he had gradually got into the doors of some major corporations. These companies kept him busy and profitable enough so that he backed away from the smaller accounts. The change really occurred about five years ago when he was able to secure a parts contract with Aerodynamics Corporation.

It came at a time when he was considering selling out and retiring. The purchase offer was generous enough to assure a secure, although modest, retirement. His wife wanted him to accept the offer, however, Joe wanted to pursue Aerodynamics. The contract was large enough that it could double his profits, and anyhow, he wasn't ready for the golf course. There was risk involved in that in order to get the contract, he would have to refinance the business to buy the necessary equipment to produce the anticipated volume. This required a second mortgage on his home and using most of the money he had put aside for retirement.

Initially, the work went well. Business volume increased significantly, but so had his debt structure. The projections had been slightly optimistic and he began having too much idle machine time on the plant floor. He knew that he should have been out looking for new customers to build up his client base, but in all honesty, he had felt too burned out and tired after so many years to beat the bushes.

So now he sat in the midst of a real crisis. Too much debt, too little business, and not enough time, ambition, or money to basically start over. How he wished he had planned for retirement and opted to sell out at the right time. The situation at hand of liquidating his equipment in order to barely pay his debts was a very depressing outcome.

Considering retirement plans

Joe Cabrella thought that he would work forever. A big mistake many small business owners make is not planning for the successful ending of their business and a sound retirement life. If you work for a large corporation, you are very interested in the type of retirement or pension program they offer. Small business owners become so absorbed with the day-to-day operations of the business that they often fail to think about or plan their retirement until it's too late. Many believe they will do fine just by selling the business when it is time to retire. Counting on this logic is extremely dangerous. You are depending on market conditions that you cannot predict.

There must be built into the profit projections of a business a method of assuring you a stable retirement. There are a number of plans you might consider.

~ **Keogh plans.** This is a retirement plan designed for the self-employed. Basically, the owner-employee can deduct 20 percent of the net income for a retirement program, not to exceed $30,000 in one year. The money is then deducted from the net earnings and taxes are not paid until the monies are withdrawn at retirement. All interest accrued on this money is also tax deferred. If a person is in the 28 percent tax bracket and earns a 9.5 percent interest return per year, it would be the equivalent of earning a 37.5 percent return the first year.

~ **IRAs.** IRAs have recently been targeted by the latest tax laws and have been vacillated. Under the current law, anyone not having a combined income of over $25,000 can set up an IRA. There are restrictions and variations. For example, if you are single and earn in excess of $35,000, and your employer has a retirement program, you are not allowed to reduce your income by making an IRA contribution. However, the interest earned on your IRA would be tax deferred.

~ **Pension plans.** A Keogh plan is a pension plan for self-employed individuals. Pension plans for corporations have different variations. There are two categories, a money purchase plan and a profit sharing plan. You are able to have 25 percent of earnings, not to exceed $30,000 deducted from current earnings on a tax-deferred basis until the money is withdrawn.

~ **Whole life insurance.** Whole life insurance plans should definitely be considered by owners of small businesses in addition to a pension plan. If you meet an early demise, it can be used to pay all outstanding debt. If you continue to live, you will redeem your entire investment plus a reasonable rate of return on the investment. It can act as additional estate value that will be additional income for your retirement years. Its interest value has grown tax deferred as well. Also, keep in mind that, as its cash value grows, it can be used as collateral for borrowing to expand the business.

An ideal business plan addresses retirement right from the start, including a method of recapturing the owner's investment. This is termed return on investment. The objective is for the owner to recover the initial monies put into the business in addition to his salary over a period of five to seven years. This money should act as seed money for retirement. If you invest $50,000 of your personal assets into a business and are able to pull an average of $7,000 to $10,000 out per year as pay-back, in addition to salary, you will have started a significant retirement program if you correctly use that money. Let's say you open a business at the age of 40. To do so, you deplete your savings or possibly your retirement reserve of $50,000. Gaining the $50,000 back at $10,000 per year for five years and putting it into a conservative investment fund would calculate as shown in Table 20–1.

Ten thousand dollars per year represents a 20 percent return on investment. Somewhat high, but so is the risk, and if it is a good idea, it can be achieved.

With this base at the age of 45, if you can put $5,000 per year into the fund and use other profits for expansion and stability of the business, 20 years later your retirement fund might look something like Table 20–2.

Not bad, particularly when you consider you might have a profitable, paid for business to sell in addition. Of course, if you are able to follow this type of program

Table 20–1.
$10,000—Five-year investment

Future value of regular deposits (annuity)

Amount of regular deposits:		$10,000.00
Are deposits made at the start of year:	Y	
Nominal interest rate:	9.500%	
Number of deposits per year:		1
Numbers of years:		5
and number of months:	0	
Future value:		$66,188.59

Year	Fund-end of period
1	10,950.00
2	22,940.26
3	36,069.59
4	50,446.20
5	66,188.59

Nominal interest rate at 9.500%.

Table 20–2.
$5,000—Twenty-Year Investment*

Future value of regular deposits (annuity)

Amount of regular deposits:	$5,000.00
Are deposits made at the start of year: Y	
Nominal interest rate: 9.500%	
Number of deposits per year:	1
Numbers of years:	20
and number of months: 0	
Future value:	$296,319.31

Year	Fund-end of period
1	5,475.00
2	11,470.13
3	18,034.79
4	25,223.10
5	33,094.30
6	41,713.25
7	51,151.02
8	61,485.36
9	72,801.48
10	85,192.63
11	98,760.91
12	113,618.21
13	129,886.95
14	147,701.20
15	167,207.83
16	188,567.55
17	211,956.47
18	237,567.34
19	265,611.25
20	296,319.31

*Nominal interest rate at 9.500%.

you might not have to sell. You might want to move into an absentee management position at a reduced salary. The other possibility pursued by many entrepreneurs is to turn it over to your children or heirs. Giving them the option to buy it from you on terms that work to their advantage is rewarding to all concerned.

Selling or retiring

Selling out a business to outsiders becomes a personal decision. There will be times when offers are made you should consider whether you are contemplating retirement or not. The idea is to sell high, not necessarily when you are ready. Try not to let your personal feelings and attachments to the business get in the way of a sound business decision. Be open to offers at anytime. The key is to put the money to proper use at the time. This might mean selling out and starting another business with part of the profits at the same time holding enough back as a reward for your efforts.

Pitfall #20 summary
Importance of insurance

The following aid is published by the Small Business Administration to explain the importance of business life insurance to the small business owner. Business life insurance provides protection for the owner-manager of a small business. When an owner-manager dies, this type of insurance can provide a financial cushion for his or her family and employees.

This aid discusses the "what's" and "why's" of business life insurance as they apply to small business owners who are involved in sole proprietorships, partnerships, or small corporations.

When the life savings of an owner-manager are invested in a small business, what happens when he or she dies? Does the business close? Does the family have to stand by and watch those savings go down the drain?

To a great extent, what happens at the owner-manager's death depends on what he or she did before that. You can protect your business and your family with business life insurance. The insurance should be tailored to your particular business and the needs of your family.

You will want to be certain that the business life insurance plan you choose covers every angle of your business. To do this, check with people who know about life insurance and your business. Among those who can help are your attorney, your accountant, your banker, and your life insurance agent or broker.

Your agent or broker can provide technical advice about the arrangement of policies. The others will give you the essential information on which your plan is based. They can also help you to see that the legal aspects are taken care of.

Purposes of insurance

Business life insurance can be written for many specific reasons. Chief among these are:

- A sole-proprietorship insurance plan to provide for maintenance of a business on the death of the sole proprietor.
- A partnership insurance plan to retire your partner's interest at death and vice versa.
- A corporation insurance plan to retire your shareholder's interest at death and vice versa.
- Key employee protection to reimburse for loss and to provide a replacement in the event of your key employee's death. Such insurance helps to prevent a setback that develops because of losing a vital employee.

- Group plan for employees. A group annuity or pension plan may be desirable where the number of employees is sufficiently large. Where only a few are involved, some form of individual retirement policy could be used, with the cost shared by employer and employees in any proportion desired.

- Reserve for emergencies. Most business life insurance plans use life insurance that has cash value. This cash value, growing over the years, provides the firm with a valuable reserve for emergencies in the event of any sharp dislocation in business conditions. When necessary, the policy cash value can be used as the basis for loans.

- Where your estate consists entirely of your interest in the business, insurance on your life, payable to your family on your death, provides them with ready cash and aids in liquidating your interest in the business.

Keep in mind when preparing a life insurance plan that too much weight should not be given to the tax angles because they are constantly changing, and a plan set up today on the basis of a certain tax advantage may prove to be disadvantageous next year. The tax factors should be left to the interpretation of the experts.

Business life insurance for sole proprietors

As mentioned earlier, life insurance protection provides an owner-manager's dependents or heirs with cash representing the sound valuation of the business at his or her death. Such insurance can also assure business continuity.

Arranging your business policy

There are several considerations that you should recognize, such as:

~ making sure that your policy adequately meets the conditions of a will or trust agreement if selling or liquidating your business is desired;

~ being aware of the need to select an appropriate beneficiary; and

~ determining who is to pay the insurance premiums.

A most important consideration is who takes "custody" of your business in case of your death. The owner-manager who does not prepare for the future leaves his or her family open for confusion and loss.

Look for problems and provide for them. For example, suppose your business is left to your son or other heir. Suppose further that the designated heir may not be capable of running the business. With your knowledge and experience, you can see friction developing among the other heirs or employees. The heir designate might also be a minor.

To solve this problem, you could consider the possibility of an executor taking over. The executor might hire a manager who might not do the best job possible because the manager realizes that the job is temporary.

If your business is transferred by sale to employees, or outsiders, there might be controversy over valuation. There might even be trouble over availability of funds to carry out the transfer.

Funds will be needed

Whichever way you choose to dispose of your business, funds will be needed—and quickly. Debts, taxes, and administrative costs have to be met. Income for your family must be provided.

Also, if your family is continuing the business, and if nobody in the family has the necessary experience, someone will probably have to be hired to manage the firm. The business will also need working capital at least for a period of readjustment. Possibly, your employees will take over the business. They will need funds for the purchase of the business, at least in part.

If your business is sold outright, working capital will be needed for the transition period. Some funds might even be needed to meet the probable discounting of assets that may accompany such a sale.

Keep in mind that the important thing is to tailor business life insurance to fit your needs. Decide what you want to happen to your firm and your family, and then plan accordingly.

Business life insurance for partnerships

Unless the partners have provided otherwise, a partnership dissolves when one of them dies. In the absence of legal safeguards to avoid dissolution, a partnership automatically dissolves at the death, or shortly after the death, of a partner. For practical purposes, the business is finished. The surviving partners become "liquidating trustees."

The only business allowed is that of winding up affairs of the partnership. If the business is continued, the surviving partners become personally liable for any losses incurred should assets not cover losses.

One way to avoid these difficulties is an adequately financed buy-and-sell agreement. Such an agreement provides for the purchase, at a prearranged valuation, of your deceased partner's interest. Your attorney can draw up the necessary papers carrying out the wishes of your partners and you.

If a buy-and-sell agreement is decided upon, the next step is to fund the arrangement, which can be done through life insurance.

Ways to set up plan

There are various ways of establishing your partnership insurance plan, each with advantages for particular requirements.

One plan involves the purchase by each partner of a policy on the life of the other partners. Each partner pays the premiums. Another plan where there are three or more partners is to have the firm buy a policy on the life of each partner.

The question of how much premiums each should pay, the amount of insurance needed, the beneficiary arrangements, tax effects, policy assignments necessary, comprise a few of the loads of questions involved.

Valuation

The valuation of your partnership is one of the most vital of all problems to be met in setting up a partnership insurance. Here you are trying to set up a formula under which full value is to be paid the deceased partner's heirs at some future time. The formula must be equitable and must satisfy all partners or it could become the basis of long-running controversy.

There are many bases of valuation. The simplest is the plan that sets an arbitrary value on each partner's interest in advance. Such a plan avoids later arguments.

It does not, however, provide for the possibly rapid shift in value through growth of the business.

If this type of plan is used, the formula for settlement could simply be a fixed valuation for goodwill, plus the net book value (current value of assets, minus liabilities).

Business life insurance for corporations

Because the success of a corporation depends largely on the abilities of the people who run it, the death of any one of them holds the possibility for financial loss to the corporation. Life insurance is useful to protect the corporation against the loss of the services of its executives. It can also provide funds for their replacement.

Corporate life insurance as it applies to small business, applies primarily to the close corporation—one with a few stockholders, all of whom are usually actively engaged in the management of the business.

Death of the principal stockholder in a close corporation might lead to management or personnel clashes that could seriously affect the business. It can cost you in the form of credit impairment, direct loss of business, or damage to your employee morale.

Unless otherwise provided, the deceased stockholder's stock becomes a part of the estate and passes into the hands of the administrator of the estate during the settlement period. The administrator can vote the stock. If it is a controlling interest, he or she could even name a new board of directors and take over full control should a principal stockholder die. Therefore, many questions are automatically raised:

- Will management deteriorate if the heirs stay in?
- Will the heirs have the ready cash needed to meet death costs?
- Can money be found by the surviving stockholders to buy out the heirs?
- Will adequate income be provided the heirs if they retain the stock?
- Can a buyer be found for the stock?
- Will the firm's credit stand up under such a strain?
- How long will the whole matter be held in controversy?
- Will the firm's sale hold up?
- Will the employees become resistive?

These are just a few of the questions that might arise. Failure to take proper steps to meet them might readily cause serious financial loss and possible bring the business to an end.

All these questions can be met and the hazard eliminated through a stock purchase and sale agreement with life insurance written into it to guarantee the funds for carrying it out. Such an agreement determines in advance just what will be done upon the death of a stockholder. It also makes funds immediately available, at that time for accomplishing the objectives of the plan.

Benefits

The benefits of having a corporate insurance plan are many. Continuity of management without interruption is guaranteed. No outsiders can come into the business unless agreed upon in advance. The cash needed to carry out the purchase of the stock is automatically provided on a basis previously agreed to as fair. The common causes of friction between heirs and surviving stockholders are removed.

Finally, widows or heirs are not burdened by business responsibilities or worries. Having a guaranteed price, they are protected against shrinking stock values.

Periodic checkup

Once an owner-manager has set up an insurance program for his or her business, he or she should check it periodically. Financial conditions change, tax laws vary in effect, and valuations of the interest of the owners are never constant—just to mention a few of the changing conditions that can affect the plan.

Revaluations should be made whenever necessary in connection with buy-and-sell agreements and partnership and corporation policies.

Changes in tax laws suggest a need for a special checkup to make certain than your tax angles are adequately covered. At least once each year, the plan should go through this careful screening by your life insurance agent or broker.

Results

A suitable business insurance program can be of value to you in many ways. It can, for instance,

~ assure immediate funds to meet taxes, debts and administrative expenses;

~ provide income for your heirs;

~ equitably distribute the property value to your heirs;

~ enable your executor, administrator, or trustee to dispose of the business to the best advantage if the family is not taking over;

~ put your family on sound financial footing if it is assuming direction of your business;

~ stabilize the credit of your business; and

~ help to maintain good employee relations by eliminating uncertainties and hazards.

Appendix A

Business plan and loan request

Name of Firm: Precision Electronics Service Company

Owner: James L. Sullivan, Sole Proprietor

Type of
Business: Small electronics service shop, repairing television sets, radios, CB radios, tape players, and other con-sumer electronics products in the shop or in the home.

Hours of
Operation: 9:00 AM – 6.00 PM (Monday through Friday)
9:00 AM – 3:00 PM (Saturday)
Closed on Sunday
On call after hours

Location
of Firm: 15 Kelly Avenue
Fort Walton Beach, FL

This location is suitable for the service type business, providing excellent accessibility from two public streets and an extra wide back entrance for unloading and loading of large items such as televisions.

The target trading area will be the greater Fort Walton Beach area, including Shalimar, Ocean City, Cinco Bayou, Mary Esther, Wright, and Eglin AFB.

BUSINESS POTENTIAL

As of January 1988, the United States had 70,526 electronic service businesses employing 207,212 technicians and providing service to an estimated 800,000,000 consumer electronics products in use today. With a 215,000,000 total U.S. population, each business serves an average population of 3,006 and 13,660 products. In Florida, there are currently 3,395 such businesses serving a population of 8,350,000, or approximately 2,460 people per business.

Considering the cosmopolitan and rather sophisticated nature of the population in this area and the growing popularity of CB radios, video games and other electronic products, it seems probable that Precision Electronics Service Company could service somewhat more people than the Florida average. Within 22 shops providing television and radio services in the Fort Walton Beach area and a total population in this area of 75,000, the average number of people serviced is 3,409 rather than the 2,460 state average.

Assuming an average of eight calls for service daily, a charge per call for both parts and labor of $20 and 26 business days per month, this would provide $4,167 in gross sales per month, or $50,000 per year.

These figures and an analysis of the local market indicate an excellent potential for this business in terms of growth, more services, and an opportunity to extend into sales of the types of products serviced.

SOURCE

National Electronic Service Dealers Association (NESDA) News Release, February 15, 1978, and NESDS newsletter.

COMPETITION:

There are 22 television and radio repair shops offering services in the Fort Walton Beach area. (See Business Potential.) However, many of these do not repair anything but televisions or radios while Precision Electronics Service Company will be able to provide services for all the items previously mentioned. There is one shop within one mile of Precision's proposed location that sells and repairs CB radios only.

SALES AND MARKETING

Recognizing that repeat customers are necessary to build a profitable business, Precision Electronics Service Company will strive to develop an image of pleasant, prompt, and courteous service as well as one of quality repair work. The business will seek to provide service both before and after the sale.

With the store remaining open until 6:00 PM on weekdays, it is hoped that this will allow customers to come in with small repair jobs after their working hours. In addition, a technician will be on call after work hours for service calls, and as an extra service, the business will provide free pickup and delivery of large items.

Initial promotion will consist of a 2-$1/2$-inch ad in the yellow pages of the phone directory, advertisements in the services classified sections of the local papers, and in the two primary free TV magazines. These advertisements will emphasize that Precision Electronics Service Company is now open for business, the types of repair services offered, and the quality of the work.

PERSONNEL

When the business is started, there will be two full-time technicians. One will be the owner and he will make withdrawals from the business rather than receiving a salary. The other technician will cost the business $10,000 the first year. One part-time clerk will be employed to do office work and take service calls. The bookkeeping and any legal work will be provided by an appropriate professional service.

SUMMARY OF LOAN APPLICATION

Applicant:	Mr. James L. Sullivan 111 Meredith Circle Fort Walton Beach, FL 32548 (904) 123-4567
Amount Requested:	$8,000
Term Requested:	Five years, no prepayment penalty at current interest rate.
Security:	Business assets, personal guarantee

Debt/Equity
Ratio After
Loan: $8,000/$16,161

Purpose
of Loan: Loan will enable applicant to start Precision Electronics
                         Service Company, an electronic service shop. The loan will
                         be used to remodel the building leased by the business,
                         purchase the necessary furniture, fixtures, and equipment,
                         and to help with start-up expenses as noted on a following
                         page.

Distribution of Loan Proceeds and Equity
30 days before opening

Use of funds	Source of funds		
	Loan	Equity	Total
Decorating and Remodeling	$1,000	$1,000	$2,000
Equipment for Repair Work	3,100	3,862	6,962
Van	3,400	2,600	6,000
		(truck trade-in)	
Initial Promotion	500	500	1,000
Office Equipment		700	700
Reserve Cash		1,000	1,000
Cash for 2 Month's Expenses		4,082	4,082
Parts Inventory		2,000	2,000
Utility and Lease Deposits		417	417
Total	$8,000	$16,000	$24,161

Collateral and Conditions

1. Security interest on all fixtures and equipment used in business.

2. Borrower will assign life insurance in the amount of the loan and keep it in force by punctual payments of required premiums.

3. Borrower will provide annual financial statements to lender.

Personal Resume

Name:	Mr. James L. Sullivan
Address:	111 Meredith Circle
	Fort Walton Beach, FL 32548
Phone:	(904) 123-4567
Personal Data:	Born: September 6, 1941
	Married
	Two children
Education:	Slater High School
	Twin Falls, Idaho
	1959
	Vocational Technical Institute
	Twin Falls, Idaho
	Television–Radio Repair Course
	Summer, 1959
	Marietta College
	Marietta, Ohio
	BA Degree in Business Administration
	1963

Employment and Business Experience:

Autoport Motel
512 North Tenth Street
Twin Falls, Idaho
Duties: Made reservations, used switchboard, kept
records
Summers during college, 1960–62

Bureau of Land Management
807 Buenavista Road
Boise, Idaho
Duties: Repaired and installed radios, supervised two
employees
1963–66

Employment and Business Experience:

Electronics Services Company
123 Fourth Avenue
Fort Walton Beach, FL 32548
Duties: Managed office, kept books and records, did some
technical work, supervised staff of five – three
technicians, two office personnel
1967–72

G&R Electronics
567 Eighth Street
Fort Walton Beach, FL 32548

Duties: Managed entire business, designed advertising, supervised sales staff of three and two technicals

1973–88

Personal Credit References:	Boggy Bayou National Bank Valparalso, FL (Check & savings)
	Bagdad Credit Union Fort Walton Beach, FL (Auto loan)
	Panhandle Mortgage Company Fort Walton Beach, FL (Real estate Loan)

Less: *Withdrawals (only if Proprietorship or Partnership)	$10,000	20%	$10,000	18.3
Undistributed profit:	$ 830	2	4,604	8.4

*Includes employer's share of social security and unemployment

Precision Electronics Service Company
Balance Sheet
(30 days before opening)

Assets
  Current Assets:
   Cash on hand and in bank $17,699

  Fixed Assets:
   Furniture, fixtures & equipment   3,862
   Truck   2,600
Total assets $24,161
Liabilities and capital
  Current Liabilities:
   Loan payable, due within 1 year $ 1,600

  Long-term Liabilities:
   Loan payable, 5 years, 9$^{1}/_{2}$ $8,000
   Less: current portion above   1,600   6,400
Total liabilities $ 8,000
Proprietor's Capital   16,161
Total liabilities and capital $24,161

Sources and Uses of Cash
Prior to opening day

Cash provided by:
  Owner's contribution $ 9,699
  Loan proceeds   8,000
  Cash available 30 days before opening $17,699
Cash to be spent prior to opening:
  Decorating and remodeling $2,000
  Equipment for repair work   3,100
  Purchase of new van (total $6,000, less
   $2,600 truck trade-in)   3,400
  Promotion prior to opening day   250
  Purchase of office equipment   700
  Purchase of parts inventory   2,000
  Utility and lease deposits   417
   Total cash expenditures prior to opening day $11,867
Cash available on opening day $ 5,832

Precision Electronics Service Company
Projected Balance Sheet
Opening Day

Assets
  Current Assets:
   Cash on hand and in bank $ 5,832

Accounts receivable	–0–	
Repair parts inventory	2,000	
Total Current Assets		$ 7,832
Fixed Assets:		
Van	$ 6,000	
Furniture, fixtures, and equipment	7,662	
Less allowance for depreciation	–0–	
Total Fixed Assets		13,662
Other Assets:		
Deposit—utilities	$ 250	
Deposit—lease	167	
Prepaid expenses—remodeling and advertising	2,250	
Total Other Assets		2,667
Total assets		$24,161
Liabilities and capital		
Current Liabilities:		
Loan payable, due within 1 year	$ 1,600	
Total Current Liabilities		$ 1,600
Long–term Liabilities:		
Loan payable, 5 years, 9¼	$8,000	
Less: Current portion above	1,600	6,400
Total Long–Term Liabilities		6,400
Total liabilities		$ 8,000
Proprietor's Capital		
Capital, beginning of period	$16,161	
Capital, end of period		16,161
Total liabilities and capital		$24,161

Precision Electronics Service Company
Projected Balance Sheet
One year after opening

Assets		
Current Assets:		
Cash on hand and in bank	$ 8,812	
Accounts receivable	–0–	
Inventory	2,000	
Total Current Assets		$10,812
Fixed Assets:		
Van	$6,000	
Furniture, fixtures & equipment	7,662	$13,662

Less accumulated depreciation	1,500	
Total Fixed Assets		12,162

Other Assets:

Deposits—utilities	$ 250	
Deposit—lease	167	
Total Other Assets		417
Total Assets		$23,391

Liabilities and capital

Current Liabilities:

Loan payable, due within 1 year	$ 1,600	
Total Current Liabilities		$ 1,600

Long—Term Liabilities:

Loan payable, 5 years, $9^1/4$	$6,400		
Less: current portion above	1,600	$ 4,800	
Total Long—Term Liabilities			4,800
Total Liabilities			$ 6,400

Proprietor's Capital

Capital, beginning of period	16,161	
Net profit for period	12,030	
Less proprietor's withdrawals	11,200	
Increase in capital		830
Capital, end of period		16,991
Total Liabilities and Capital		$23,391

Balance Sheet Explanations
Opening Day

Cash: $17,699 available 30 days before   Furniture, Fixtures, Equip.

Less:	2,000 remodeling
	3,100 equipment
	3,400 van
	700 office equipment
	417 utility and lease deposits
	2,000 inventory
	250 advertising in advance
	$ 5,832 Cash on opening day

$ 6,962	equip. for repair work
700	office equipment
$ 7,662	

All cash expenditures prior to opening have been converted into assets. Thus, the proprietor's capital remains the same. Unlike the other cash expenditures, the $250 in advertising and $2,000 in decorating/remodeling are "temporary assets." (See Prepaid Expenses under Other Assets.) Once the business is open, these assets will be transferred to an expense account and will appear in the Income statement. Therefore, so as not to make a double charge, cash of $2,250 is included in the balance sheet for one year after opening.

One Year After Opening

Cash:	$ 5,832	available on opening day
Less:	1,600	loan payment
Plus:	830	undistributed profit
	1,500	depreciation (not a cash expense)
	2,250	remodeling/advertising (see note above)
	$ 8,812	Cash one year after opening

Appendix B

Corporate bylaws

BYLAWS

OF

_____

ARTICLE I. OFFICES

<u>Section 1</u>. <u>Principal Office</u>. The principal office for the transaction of the business of the corporation shall be located at such place as may be fixed from time to time by the Board of Directors.

<u>Section 2</u>. <u>Other Offices</u>. Branch offices and places of business may be established at any time by the Board of Directors at any place or places where the corporation is qualified to do business, whether within or without the State of Georgia.

ARTICLE II. SHAREHOLDERS' MEETINGS

<u>Section 1</u>. <u>Meetings, Where Held</u>. Any meeting of the shareholders of the corporation, whether an annual meeting or a special meeting, may be held either at the principal office of the corporation or at any place in the United States within or without the State of Georgia.

169

Section 2.   Annual Meeting. The annual meeting of the shareholders of the corporation shall be held on the third Tuesday of the third month following the end of the fiscal year of the corporation; provided, that if said day shall fall upon a legal holiday, then such annual meeting shall be held on the next day thereafter ensuing which is not a legal holiday. At an annual meeting of shareholders, any matter relating to the affairs of the corporation, whether or not stated in the notice of the meeting, may be brought up for action except matters which the Georgia Business Corporation Code requires to be stated in the notice of the meeting.

Section 3.   Special Meetings. A special meeting of the shareholders, for any purpose or purposes whatsoever, may be called at any time by the Chairman of the Board, President, Vice President, a majority of the Board, President, Vice President, a majority of the Board of Directors, or one or more shareholders holding not less than one-third of the voting power of the corporation. Such a call for a special meeting must state the purpose of the meeting.

Section 4.   Notice of Meetings. Unless waived, written notice stating the place, day and hour of each meeting, and, in the case of a special meeting, the purpose or purposes for which the meeting is called, shall be delivered to each shareholder not less than ten days (or not less than any such other minimum period of days as may be prescribed by the Georgia Business Corporation Code) nor more than fifty days before the date of the meeting either personally or by first class mail by, or at the direction of, the directors, the President, the Secretary or the officer or persons calling the meeting. If mailed, such notice shall be deemed to be delivered when deposited in the United States mail with first class postage thereon prepaid, addressed to the shareholder at his address as it appears on the stock transfer books of the corporation. The notice of any annual or special meeting shall also include, or be accompanied by, any additional statements, information, or documents prescribed by the Georgia Business Corporation Code. When a meeting is adjourned to another time or place, it shall not be necessary to give any notice of the adjourned meeting if the time and place to which the meeting is adjourned are announced at the meeting at which the adjournment is taken, and at the adjourned meeting any business may be transacted that might have been transacted on the original date of the meeting. If, however, after the adjournment the Board fixes a new record date for the adjourned meeting, a notice of the adjourned meeting shall be given to each shareholder on the new record date.

Section 5.   Waiver of Notice. Notice of any annual or special meeting may be waived by any shareholder, either before or after the meeting; and the attendance of a shareholder at a meeting, either in person or by proxy, shall of itself constitute waiver of notice and waiver of any and all objections to the place or time of the meeting, or to the manner in which it has been called or convened, except when a shareholder attends solely for the purpose of stating, at the beginning of the meeting, an objection or objections to the transaction of business at such meeting.

Section 6.   Quorum, Voting and Proxy. Shareholders representing a majority of the common stock issued and outstanding shall constitute a quorum at a shareholders' meeting. If a quorum is present, the affirmative vote of the majority of the shares represented at the meeting and entitled to vote on the subject matter shall be the act of the shareholders, unless the vote of a greater number of voting by classes or series is required by the Articles of Incorporation or by the Georgia Business Corporation Code. Each common shareholder shall be entitled to one vote for each share of common stock owned. Any shareholder who is entitled to attend a shareholders' meeting, to vote thereat, or to execute consents, waivers, or releases, may be represented at such meeting or vote thereat, and execute consents, waivers, and releases, and exercise any of his other rights, by one or more agents, who may be either an individual or individuals or any domestic or foreign corporation, authorized by a written proxy executed by such person or by his attorney-in-fact. A telegram or cablegram transmitted by a shareholder shall be deemed a written proxy. No proxy shall be valid after the expiration of eleven months from the date thereof unless otherwise provided in the proxy. Every proxy shall be revocable at the pleasure of the person executing it, except as otherwise provided by the Georgia Business Corporation Code. If a proxy expressly provides, any proxy holder may appoint in writing a substitute to act in his place.

Section 7.   No Meeting Necessary, When. Any action required by law or permitted to be taken at any shareholders' meeting may be taken without a meeting if written consent, setting forth the action so taken, shall be signed by all shareholders entitled to vote with respect to the subject matter thereof. Such consent shall have the same force and effect as a unanimous vote of the shareholders and shall be filed with the Secretary and recorded in the Minute Book of the corporation.

ARTICLE III.   BOARD OF DIRECTORS

Section 1.   Functions and Definitions. The business and affairs of the corporation shall be managed by a governing board, which is herein referred to as the "Board of Directors" or "directors" notwithstanding that only one director legally constitutes the Board. The use of the phrase "entire Board" or "full Board" in these Bylaws refers to the total number of directors which the corporation would have if there were no vacancies.

Section 2.   Qualifications and Number. Each director shall be at least twenty-one years of age. A director need not be a shareholder, a citizen of the United States or a resident of the State of Georgia. The initial Board of Directors shall consist of the directors fixed in the Articles of Incorporation. Thereafter, the number of directors constituting the entire board shall be not less than three nor more than fifteen members, except that, where all the shares are owned beneficially and of record by less than three shareholders, the number of directors may be less than three but not less than the number of such shareholders. Subject to the foregoing limitation, the precise number of directors is to be fixed by a resolution of the shareholders from time to time. No decrease in the number of directors shall have the effect of shortening the term of any incumbent director.

Section 3.   Election and Tenure. Each director named as such in the Articles of Incorporation shall hold office until the first annual meeting of shareholders and until his successor is elected and qualified, or until his earlier resignation, removal from office, or death. At the first annual meeting of the shareholders and at each annual meeting thereafter, directors shall be elected, and each shall hold office until the next annual meeting of shareholders and until their successors are elected and qualified, or until their earlier resignation, removal from office, or death. In such elections, the persons having a plurality of votes shall be elected.

Section 4.   Powers. The Board of Directors shall have authority to manage the affairs and exercise the powers, privileges and franchises of the corporation as they may deem expedient for the interests of the corporation, subject to the terms of the Articles of Incorporation, bylaws, any valid Shareholders' Agreement, and such policies and directions as may be prescribed from time to time by the shareholders.

Section 5.   Meetings. The annual meeting of the Board of Directors shall be held without notice immediately following the annual meeting of the shareholders, on the same date and at the same place as said annual meeting of the shareholders. The Board by resolution may provide for regular meetings, which may be held without notice as and when scheduled in such resolution. Special meetings of the Board may be called at any time by the Chairman of the Board, the President, or by any two or more directors. The Board of Directors, or any committee designated by the Board of Directors, may participate in a meeting of such Board or committee by means of conference telephone or similar communications equipment in which all persons participating in the meeting can hear each other; and participation in such a meeting pursuant to this Section 5 shall constitute presence in person at such meeting.

Section 6.   Notice and Waiver; Quorum. Notice of any special meeting of the Board of Directors shall be given to each director personally or by mail, telegram or cablegram addressed to him at his last known address, at least one day prior to the meeting. Such notice may be waived, either before or after the meeting; and the attendance of a director at any special meeting shall of itself constitute a waiver of notice of such meeting and of any and all objections to the place or time of the meeting, or to the manner in which it has been called or convened, except where a director states, at the beginning of the meeting, any such objection or objections to the transaction of business. A majority of the Board of Directors shall constitute a quorum at any directors' meeting.

Section 7.   No Meeting Necessary, When. Any action required by law or permitted to be taken at any meeting of the Board of Directors may be taken without a meeting if written consent, setting forth the action so taken, shall be signed by all the directors. Such consent shall have the same force and effect as a unanimous vote of the Board of Directors and shall be filed with the Secretary and recorded in the Minute Book of the corporation.

Section 8.   Voting. At all meetings of the Board of Directors each director shall have one vote and, except as otherwise provided herein or provided by law, all questions shall be determined by a majority vote of the directors present.

Section 9.   Removal. Any one or more directors or the entire Board of Directors may be removed from office, with or without cause, by the affirmative vote of the holders of a majority of the shares entitled to vote at any shareholders' meeting with respect to which notice of such purpose has been given.

Section 10.   Vacancies. Any vacancy occurring in the Board of Directors shall be filled by the affirmative vote of a majority of the remaining directors, even though less than a quorum, or by the sole remaining directors, as the case may be, or by the shareholders if the vacancy is not so filled or if no director remains, and when so filled such appointee shall serve for the unexpired term of the director to whose place he succeeds.

Section 11.   Dividends. The Board of Directors may declare dividends payable in cash or other property out of the unreserved and unrestricted net earnings of the current fiscal year, computed to the date of declaration of the dividend, or the preceding fiscal year, or out of the unreserved and unrestricted earned surplus of the corporation, or out of the unreserved and unrestricted capital surplus if so authorized by the Articles of Incorporation, as they may deem expedient.

Section 12.   Committees. In the discretion of the Board of Directors, said Board from time to time may elect or appoint, from its own members, an Executive Committee or such other committee or committees as said Board may see fit to establish. Each such committee shall consist of two or more directors, and each shall have and may exercise such authority and perform such functions as the Board by resolution may prescribe within the limitations imposed by law.

Section 13.   Officers, Salaries and Bonds. The Board of Directors shall elect all officers of the corporation and fix their compensation, unless pursuant to resolution of the Board the authority to fix compensation is delegated to the President. The fact that any officer is a director shall not preclude him from receiving a salary or from voting upon the resolution providing the same. The Board of Directors may or may not, in their discretion, require bonds from either or all of the officers and employees of the corporation for the faithful performance of their duties and good conduct while in office.

Section 14.   Compensation of Directors. Directors, as such, shall be entitled to receive such fees and expenses, if any, for attendance at each regular or special meeting of the Board and any adjournments thereof, as may be fixed from time to time by resolution of the Board, and such fees and expenses shall be payable even though an adjournment be had because of the absence of a quorum; provided, however, that nothing herein contained shall be construed to preclude any director from serving the corporation in any other capacity and receiving compensation therefor. Members of either standing or special committees may be allowed such compensation as may be provided from time to time by resolution of the Board for attending committee meetings.

ARTICLE IV.   OFFICERS

Section 1.   Selection. The Board of Directors at each annual meeting shall elect or appoint a President (who shall be a director), a Secretary and a Treasurer, each to serve for the ensuing year and until his successor is elected and qualified, or until his earlier resignation, removal from office, or death. The Board of Directors, at such meeting, may or may not, in the discretion of the Board, elect a Chairman of the Board and/or one or more Vice Presidents and, also may elect or appoint one or more Assistant Vice Presidents and/or one or more Assistant Secretaries and/or one or more Assistant Treasurers. When more than one Vice President is elected, they may, in the discretion of the Board, be designated Executive Vice President, First Vice President, Second Vice President, etc., according to seniority or rank, and any person may hold two or more offices except that the President shall not also serve as the Secretary.

Section 2.   Removal, Vacancies. Any officers of the corporation may be removed from office at any time by the Board of Directors, with or without cause. Any vacancy occurring in any office of the corporation may be filled by the Board of Directors.

Section 3.   Chairman of the Board. The Chairman of the Board of Directors, when and if elected, shall whenever present, preside at all meetings of the Board of Directors and at all meetings of the shareholders. The Chairman of the Board of Directors shall have all the powers of the President in the event of his absence or inability to act, or in the event of a vacancy in the office of the President. The Chairman of the Board of Directors shall confer with the President on matters of general policy affecting the business of the corporation and shall have, in his discretion, power and authority to generally supervise all the affairs of the corporation and the acts and conduct of all the officers of the corporation, and shall have such other duties as may be conferred upon the Chairman of the Board by the Board of Directors.

Section 4.   President. If there be no Chairman of the Board elected, or in his absence, the President shall preside at all meetings of the Board of Directors and at all meetings of the shareholders. The immediate supervision of the affairs of the corporation shall be vested in the President. It shall be his duty to attend constantly to the business of the corporation and maintain strict supervision over all of its affairs and interests. He shall keep the Board of Directors fully advised of the affairs and condition of the corporation, and shall manage and operate the business of the corporation pursuant to such policies as may be prescribed from time to time by the Board of Directors. The President shall, subject to approval of the Board, hire and fix the compensation of all employees and agents of the corporation other than officers, and any person thus hired shall be removable at his pleasure.

Section 5.   Vice President. Any Vice President of the corporation may be designated by the Board of Directors to act for and in the place of the President in the event of sickness, disability or absence of said President or the failure of said President to act for any reason, and when so designated, such Vice President shall exercise all the powers of the President in accordance with such designation. The Vice Presidents shall have such duties as may be required of, or assigned to, them by the Board of Directors, Chairman of the Board or the President.

Section 6.   Secretary. It shall be the duty of the Secretary to keep a record of the proceedings of all meetings of the shareholders and Board of Directors; to keep the stock records of the corporation; to notify the shareholders and directors of meetings as provided by these bylaws; and to perform such other duties as may be prescribed by the Chairman of the Board, President or Board of Directors. Any Assistant Secretary, if elected, shall perform the duties of the Secretary during the absence or disability of the Secretary and shall perform such other duties as may be prescribed by the Chairman of the Board, President, Secretary or Board of Directors.

Section 7.   Treasurer. The Treasurer shall keep, or cause to be kept, the financial books and records of the corporation, and shall faithfully account for its funds. He shall make such reports as may be necessary to keep the Chairman of the Board, the President and Board of Directors fully informed at all times as to the financial condition of the corporation, and shall perform such other duties as may be prescribed by the Chairman of the Board, President or Board of Directors. Any Assistant Treasurer, if elected, shall perform the duties of the Treasurer during the absence or disability of the Treasurer, and shall perform such other duties as may be prescribed by the Chairman of the Board, President, Treasurer or Board of Directors.

ARTICLE V.   CONTRACTS, ETC.

Section 1.   Contracts, Deeds and Loans. All contracts, deeds, mortgages, pledges, promissory notes, transfers and other written instruments binding upon the corporation shall be executed on behalf of the corporation by the Chairman of the Board, if elected, the President, any Vice President, or by such other officers or agents as the Board of Directors may designate from time to time. Any such instrument required to be given under the seal of the corporation may be attested by the Secretary or Assistant Secretary of the corporation.

Section 2.   Proxies. The Chairman of the Board, if elected, or the President or any Vice President shall have full power and authority, on behalf of the corporation, to attend and to act and to vote at any meetings of the shareholders, bond holders or other security holders of any corporation, trust or association in which this corporation may hold securities, and at any such meeting shall possess and may exercise any and all of the rights and powers inciden to the ownership of such securities and which as owner thereof the corporation might have possessed and exercised if present, including the power and authority to delegate such power and authority to a proxy selected by him. The Board of Directors may, by resolution, from time to time, confer like powers upon any other person or persons.

ARTICLE VI.   CHECKS AND DRAFTS

Checks and drafts of the corporation shall be signed by such officer or officers or such other employees or persons as the Board of Directors may from time to time designate.

ARTICLE VII.   STOCK

Section 1.   Certificates of Stock. The certificates for shares of capital stock of the corporation shall be in such form as shall be determined by the Board of Directors. They shall be numbered consecutively and entered into the stock book of the corporation as they are issued. Each certificate shall state on its face the fact that the corporation is a Georgia corporation, the name of the person to whom the shares are issued, the number and class of shares (and series, if any) represented by the certificate and their par value, or a statement that they are without par value. In addition, when and if more than one class of shares shall be outstanding, all share certificates of whatever class shall state that the corporation will furnish to any shareholder upon request and without charge a full statement of the designations, relative rights, preferences and limitations of the shares of each class authorized to be issued by the corporation.

Section 2.   <u>Signature; Transfer Agent; Registrar</u>. Share certificates
shall be signed by the Chairman of the Board, the President or any Vice
President and by the Treasurer or an Assistant Treasurer, or the Secretary
or an Assistant Secretary of the corporation, and shall bear the seal of the
corporation or a facsimile thereof. The Board of Directors may from time to
time appoint transfer agents and registrars for the shares of capital stock
of the corporation or any class thereof, and when any share certificate is
countersigned by a transfer agent or registered by a registrar, the
signature of any officer of the corporation appearing thereon may be a
facsimile signature. In case any officer who signed, or whose facsimile
signature was placed upon, any such certificate shall have died or ceased to
be such officer before such certificate is issued, it may nevertheless be
issued with the same effect as if he continued to be such officer on the date
of issue.

Section 3.   <u>Stock Book</u>. The corporation shall keep at its principal office,
or at the office of its transfer agent, wherever located, with a copy at the
principal office of the corporation, a book, to be known as the stock book of
the corporation, containing in alphabetical order the name of each
shareholder of record, together with his address, the number of shares of
each kind, class or series of stock held by him and his social security
number. The stock book shall be maintained in current condition. The stock
book, including the share register, or the duplicate copy thereof
maintained at the principal office of the corporation, shall be available
for inspection and copying by any shareholder at any meeting of the
shareholders upon request, or at other times upon the written request of any
shareholder or holder of a voting trust certificate. The stock book may be
inspected and copied either by a shareholder or a holder of a voting trust
certificate in person, or by their duly authorized attorney or agent. The
information contained in the stock book and share register may be stored on
punch cards, magnetic tape, or any other approved information storage
devices related to electronic data processing equipment, provided that any
such method, device, or system employed shall first be approved by the Board
of Directors, and provided further that the same is capable of reproducing
all information contained therein, in legible and understandable form, for
inspection by shareholders or for any other proper corporate purpose.

Section 4.   <u>Transfer of Stock; Registration of Transfer</u>. The stock of the
corporation shall be transferred only by surrender of the certificate and
transfer upon the stock book of the corporation. Upon surrender to the
corporation, or to any transfer agent or registrar for the class of shares
represented by the certificate surrendered, of a certificate properly
endorsed for transfer, accompanied by such assurances as the corporation,
or such transfer agent or registrar, may require as to the genuineness and
effectiveness of each necessary endorsement and satisfactory evidence of
compliance with all applicable laws relating to securities transfers and
the collection of taxes, it shall be the duty of the corporation, or such

transfer agent or registrar, to issue a new certificate, cancel the old certificate and record the transactions upon the stock book of the corporation.

Section 5.   Registered Shareholders. Except as otherwise required by law, the corporation shall be entitled to treat the person registered on its stock book as the owner of shares of capital stock of the corporation as the person exclusively entitled to receive notification, dividends or other distributions, to vote and to otherwise exercise all the rights and powers of ownership and shall not be bound to recognize any adverse claim.

Section 6.   Record Date. For the purpose of determining shareholders entitled to notice of or to vote at any meeting of shareholders or any adjournment thereof, or to express consent to or dissent from any proposal without a meeting, or for the purpose of determining shareholders entitled to receive payment of any dividend or the allotment of any rights, or for the purpose of any other action affecting the interests or shareholders, the Board of Directors may fix, in advance, a record date. Such date shall not be more than fifty (50) nor less than ten (10) days before the date of any such meeting nor more than fifty (50) days prior to any other action. In each case, except as otherwise provided by law, only such persons as shall be shareholders of record on the date so fixed shall be entitled to notice of and to vote at such meeting and any adjournment thereof, to express such consent or dissent, or to receive payment of such dividend or such allotment of rights, or otherwise be recognized as shareholders for any other related purpose, notwithstanding any registration of a transfer of shares on the stock book of the corporation after any such record date so fixed.

Section 7.   Lost Certificates. When a person to whom a certificate of stock has been issued alleges it to have been lost, destroyed or wrongfully taken, and if the corporation, transfer agent or registrar is not on notice that such certificate has been acquired by bona fide purchaser, a new certificate may be issued upon such owner's compliance with all of the following conditions, to—wit: (a) He shall file with the Secretary of the corporation, and the transfer agent or the registrar, his request for the issuance of a new certificate, with an affidavit setting forth the time, place, and circumstances of the loss; (b) He shall also file with the Secretary, and the transfer agent or the registrar, a bond with good and sufficient security acceptable to the corporation and the transfer agent or the registrar, conditioned to indemnify and save harmless the corporation and the transfer agent or the registrar from any and all damage, liability and expense of every nature whatsoever resulting from the corporation's or the transfer agent's or the registrar's issuing a new certificate in place of the one alleged to have been lost; and (c) He shall comply with such other reasonable requirements as the Chairman of the Board, the President, or the Board of Directors of the corporation, and the transfer agent or the registrar shall deem appropriate under the circumstances.

Section 8.   Replacement of Mutilated Certificates. A new certificate may be issued in lieu of any certificate previously issued that may be defaced or mutilated upon surrender for cancellation of a part of the old certificate sufficient in the opinion of the Secretary and the transfer agent or the registrar to duly identify the defaced or mutilated certificate and to protect the corporation and the transfer agent or the registrar against loss or liability. Where sufficient identification is lacking, a new certificate may be issued upon compliance with all of the conditions set forth in Section 7 of this Article VII.

ARTICLE VIII.   INDEMNIFICATION

Section 1.   General. Under the circumstances prescribed in Sections 3 and 4 of this Article, the corporation shall indemnify and hold harmless any person who was or is a party or is threatened to be made a party to any threatened, pending or completed action, suit or proceeding, whether civil, criminal, administrative or investigative (other than an action by or in the right of the corporation) by reason of the fact that he is or was a director, officer, employee or agent of the corporation, or is or was serving at the request of the corporation as a director, officer, employee or agent of another corporation, partnership, joint venture, trust or other enterprise, against expenses (including attorneys' fees), judgments, fines and amounts paid in settlement actually and reasonably incurred by him in connection with such action, suit or proceeding if he acted in a manner he reasonably believed to be in, or not opposed to, the best interests of the corporation, and with respect to any criminal action or proceeding, had no reasonable cause to believe his conduct was unlawful. The termination of any action, suit or proceeding by judgment order, settlement, conviction, or upon a plea of nolo contendere or its equivalent, shall not, of itself, create a presumption that the person did not act in a manner which he reasonably believed to be in, or not opposed to, the best interest of the corporation, and with respect to any criminal action or proceeding, had reasonable cause to believe that his conduct was unlawful.

Section 2.   Action In the Right of the Corporation. Under the circumstances prescribed in Sections 3 and 4 or this Article, the corporation shall indemnify and hold harmless any person who was or is a party or is threatened to be made a party to any threatened, pending or completed action or suit by or in the right of the corporation to procure a judgment in its favor by reason of the fact he is or was a director, officer, employee or age of the corporation, or is or was serving at the request of the corporation as a director, officer, employee or agent of another corporation, partnership, joint venture, trust or other enterprise, against expenses (including attorneys' fees) actually and reasonably incurred by him in connection with the defense or settlement of such action or suit, if he acted in good faith and in a manner he reasonably believed to be in or not opposed to the best interests of the corporation, except that no indemnification shall be made in respect to any claim, issue or matter as to which such person shall have been adjudged to be liable for the negligence or misconduct in the performance of his duty to the corporation, unless, and only to the extent that, the court' in which such action or suit was brought shall determine upon application that, despite the adjudication of liability but in view of all the circumstances of the case, such person is fairly and reasonably entitled to idemnity for such expenses which the court shall deem proper.

Section 3.   Conditions to Indemnification. To the extent that a director, officer, employee or agent of the corporation has been successful on the merits, or otherwise, in defense of any action, suit or proceeding referred to in Sections 1 and 2 of this Article, or in defense of any claim, issue or matter therein, he shall be indemnified against expenses (including attorneys' fees) actually and reasonably incurred by him in connection therewith.

Section 4.   Determination By Corporation. Except as provided in Section 3 of this Article and except as may be ordered by a court, any indemnification under Sections 1 and 2 of this Article shall be made by the corporation only as authorized in the specific case upon a determination that indemnification of the director, officer, employee or agent is proper in the circumstances because he has met the applicable standard of conduct set forth in Sections 1 and 2. Such determination shall be made (1) by the Board of Directors by a majority vote of a quorum consisting of directors who were not parties to such action, suit or proceeding, or (2) if such a quorum is not obtainable, or, even if obtainable, if a quorum of disinterested directors so directs, by the firm of independent legal counsel then employed by the corporation, in a written opinion, or (3) by the affirmative vote of a majority of the share entitled to vote thereon.

Section 5.   Advance Payment. Expenses incurred in defending a civil or criminal action, suit or proceeding may be paid by the corporation in advance of the final disposition of such action, suit or proceeding as authorized by the Board of Directors in the specific case upon receipt of an undertaking by or on behalf of the director, officer, employee or agent to repay such amount unless it shall ultimately be determined that he is entitled to be indemnified by the corporation as authorized in this Article VIII.

Section 6.   Nonexclusive Remedy. The indemnification provided by this Article VIII shall not be deemed exclusive of any other rights, in respect of indemnification or otherwise, to which those seeking indemnification may be entitled under any bylaw or resolution approved by the affirmative vote of the holders of a majority of the shares entitled to vote therein taken at a meeting the notice of which specified that such bylaw or resolution would be placed before the shareholders, both as to action by a

director, officer, employee, or agent in his official capacity and as to
action in another capacity while holding such ofice or position, and shall
continue as to a person who has ceased to be a director, officer, employee or
agent and shall inure to the benefit of the heirs, executors or
administrators of such a person.

Section 7.   Insurance. The corporation may purchase and maintain insurance
on behalf of any person who is or was a director, officer, employee or agent
of the corporation, or is or was serving at the request of the corporation,
as a director, officer, employee or agent of another corporation,
partnership, joint venture, trust or other enterprise, against any
liability asserted against him and incurred by him in any such capacity, or
arising out of his status as such, whether or not the corporation would have
the power to indemnify him against such liability under the provisions of
this Article VIII.

Section 8.   Notice to Shareholders. If any expenses or other amounts are
paid by way of indemnification, otherwise than by court order or by an
insurance carrier pursuant to insurance maintained by the corporation, the
corporation shall, unless such meeting is held within three months from the
date of such payment, and, in any event, within fifteen months from the date
of such payment, send by first class mail to its shareholders of record at
the time entitled to vote for the election of directors, a statement
specifying the persons paid, the amounts paid, and the nature and status at
the time of such payment of the litigation or threatened litigation.

Section 9.   Miscellaneous. For purposes of Sections 1 and 2 of this Article
VIII, reference to "the corporation" shall include, in addition to the
corporation, any merging or consolidating corporation (including any
merging or consolidating corporation of a merging or consolidating
corporation) absorbed in a merger or consolidation with the corporation so
that any person who is or was a director, officer, employee or agent of such
merging or consolidating corporation, or is or was serving at the request of
such merging or consolidating corporation as a director, officer, employee
or agent of another corporation, partnership, joint venture, trust or other
enterprise, shall stand in the same position under the provisions of
Sections 1 and 2 of this Article VIII with respect to the corporation as he
would if he had served the corporation in the same capacity; provided,
however, no indemnification under Sections 1 and 2 of this Article VIII as
permitted by this Section 9 shall be mandatory under this Section 9 without
the approval of such indemnification by the Board of Directors or
shareholders of the corporation in the manner provided in Section 4 of this
Article VIII.

ARTICLE IX.   REIMBURSEMENT BY CORPORATE EMPLOYEES

Any payments made to an employee of the corporation in the form of a salary
or bonus payment which shall be disallowed, in whole or in part, as a

deductible expense to the corporation for Federal or State income tax purposes by the Internal Revenue Service, or by the State Revenue Department, shall be reimbursed by such employee to the corporation to the full extent of such disallowance within six (6) months after the date on which the corporation pays the deficiency with respect to such disallowance. It shall be the duty of the Board of Directors of the corporation to enforce payment to the corporation by any such employee for the amount disallowed. The corporation shall not be required to legally defend any proposed disallowance by the Internal Revenue Service or by the State Revenue Department, and the amount required to be reimbursed by such employee shall be the amount, as finally determined by agreement or otherwise, which is actually disallowed as a deduction. In lieu of payment to the corporation by any such employee, the Board of Directors may, in the discretion of the Board, withhold amounts from such employee's future compensation payments until the amount owed to the corporation has been fully recovered.

ARTICLE X.   AMENDMENT

The Board of Directors shall have the power to alter, amend or repeal the bylaws or adopt new bylaws unless such power is reserved exclusively to the shareholders by the Articles of Incorporation or in bylaws previously adopted by shareholders, but any bylaws adopted by the Board of Directors may be altered, amended or repealed, and new bylaws adopted, by the shareholders. The shareholders may prescribe that any bylaw or bylaws adopted by them shall not be altered, amended or repealed by the Board of Directors.

SUBSCRIPTION AGREEMENT

_____ (the "Subscribers") hereby agree as follows:

1. The Subscribers hereby agree to subscribe for and to purchase the number of shares of $_____ par value common stock of _____ (the "Corporation") set forth opposite their respective names below, pursuant to the Corporation's "Plan to Issue 1244 Stock" to be adopted at the organizational meeting of the Board of Directors of the Corporation.

Name	Number of Shares	Cash Consideration	Consideration Other Than Cash	Total Consideration

2. Upon the acceptance of this Subscription Agreement by the Corporation, the Subscribers agree to pay or deliver to the Corporation the consideration indicated above in exchange for the issuance by the Corporation of the number of shares of common stock herein subscribed for.

Executed this ____ day of _____, 198__.

_____

_____

Accepted this ____ day of _____, 198__.

_____

By _____
   President

To: _____
   _____
   _____

Re: Purchase of _____ shares of
   the $_____ par value common
   stock (the "securities") of

   _____
   (the "Company")

Pursuant to a Stock Subscription Agreement of even date herewith, the undersigned is purchasing securities of the Company as set forth in the caption hereto. The undersigned understands and recognizes that the securities to be issued by the Company and purchased by the undersigned pursuant to the aforementioned Stock Subscription Agreement are to be so issued and purchased without registration under the Securities Act of 1933, as amended (the "Securities Act"), in reliance upon the exemption contained in Section 4(2) of the Securities Act and without registration under the Georgia Securities Act of 1973, as amended (the "Georgia Act"), in reliance upon the exemption contained in Section 9(m) of the Georgia Act. In order to comply with and protect and preserve the foregoing registration exemptions under the Securities Act and the Georgia Act:

(1) The undersigned represents that the undersigned is purchasing the securities for investment only solely for the undersigned's account with no intent of or view to directly or indirectly participating in a distribhution of the securities;

(2) The undersigned agrees that none of the securities may be transferred, sold, exchanged, pledged, hypothecated or otherwise disposed of unless any necessary registration statement under the Securities Act and/or the Georgia Act is then in effect as to the securities or unless the prior written approval of counsel for the Company is obtained stating that the transaction is exempt from registration under the Securities Act and the Georgia Act—the Company represents that such written approval from its counsel shall not be unreasonably withheld and that the basis of consideration for such written approval shall be compliance with the requirements of the Securities Act and the Georgia Act regarding the continuing applicability of the aforementioned registration exemptions to the Company's original offering and issuance of the securities; and

(3) The undersigned agrees to the placement of a legend upon the stock certificates evidencing the securities to the effect that the securities may not be transferred, sold, exchanged, hypothecated or otherwise disposed of unless any necessary registration statement under the Securities Act and/or the Georgia Act is then in effect as to the securities or unless the prior written approval of counsel for the Company is obtained stating that the transaction is exempt from registration under said Acts.

This _____ day of _____ , 199__.

_____

As to the Company's representation with regard to the opinion letter of its counsel, this _____ day of _____ , 199__.

_____

By _____
                                    President

RESTRICTIVE LEGEND

The shares evidenced by this certificate have been acquired for investment and have not been registered under the Georgia Securities Act of

1973, as amended (the "Georgia Act"), in reliance upon the exemption contained in Section 9(m) of the Georgia Act, or under the Securities Act of 1933, as amended (the "1933 Act"), in reliance upon the exemptions contained in Section 4(2) or Section 3(a)(11) of the 1933 Act. These shares may not be sold or transferred except in transactions (a) registered under the 1933 Act, or exempt from registration thereunder, and (b) registered under the Georgia Act, or exempt from registration thereunder, or otherwise in compliance with the Georgia Act.

Bibliography

Small business management

Bangs, David H., Jr. *The Cash Flow Control Guide: Methods to Understand & Control Small Business's Number One Problem*. Upstart Publishing, 1989.

Bangs, David H., Jr. *The Start Up Guide: A One Year Plan for Entrepreneurs*. Upstart Publishing, 1989.

Barreto, Humberto. *The Entrepreneur in Micro-Economic Theory: Disappearance & Explanation*. Routledge Chapman & Halkl, 1989.

Baumback, Clifford M. *How to Organize & Operate a Small Business*. Prentice Hall, 1988.

Berger, Lisa; Berger, Donelson; Eastwood, C. William. *Cashing In: Getting the Most when You Sell your Business*. Warner Books, 1989.

Berle, Gustav. *Business Book*. Wiley, 1989.

Bevers, Charles; Christie, Linda; Price, Lynn R. *The Entrepreneur's Guide to Doing Business with the Federal Government: A Guide for Small & Growing Businesses*. Prentice Hall Press, 1989.

Bird, Barbara J. *Entrepreneurial Behavior*. Scott F, 1989.

Burstiner, Irving. *The Small Business Handbook: A Comprehensive Guide to Starting and Running Your Own Business*. Prentice Hall Press, 1989.

Burton. *Owners Manual: Operating Instruction for Profitable Business*. Wiley, 1988.

Carpenter, Donna S. *Laventhol & Horwath Planning Guide for Small Business Owners & Professionals*. Bantam, 1987.

Carpenter, Gene C. *One Thousand One Business Anyone Can Start or Buy*. Trend Publication, 1988.

Center for Innovation & Business Development Staff. *Entrepreneur Kit: The Business Plan*. Lord Publishing, 1988.

Cook, James R. *The Start-up Entrepreneur: How You Can Succeed in Building Your Own Company Into a Major Enterprise Starting From Scratch*. Harper Row, 1987.

Deleon, Benjamin. *Entrepreneurship: The Supercareer of the Nineties*. Papermate Publishing, 1990.

DeYoung, John. *Cases in Small Management: A Strategic Problems Approach*. Merrill, 1988.

Dichter, David; Husbands, Robert; Areson, Ann; and Frey, Mark. *A Guide to Technology Transfer for Small and Medium-Sized Enterprises*. Gower Publishing Co., 1988.

Faber, Peter L.; Holbrook, Martin E. *S Corporation Manual: A Special Tax Break for Small Business Corporations*. Prentice Hall, 1988.

Giersch, Herbert-Editor. *New Opportunities for Entrepreneurship: International Perspectives*. Westview, 1988.

Goldstein, Arnold S.-Editor. *J. K. Lasser's Complete Legal Form-File for Small Business*. S&S, 1988.

Goldstein, Arnold S. *Buying and Selling a Business Successfully: A Proven Guide for Entrepreneurs*. Dow Jones Irwin, 1989.

Gregory, H.; Winter, Barbara J.-Frwd. by. *Finding & Keeping Customers: A Small Business Handbook*. Pinstripe Publishing, 1989.

Halloran, James W. *The Entrepreneur's Guide to Starting a Successful Business*. TAB BOOKS, 1987.

Hawken, Paul. *Growing A Business*. S&S, 1988.

Hisrich, Peters. *Entrepreneurship*. Irwin, 1989.

Hodgetts, Richard M.; Kuratko, Donald F. *Effective Small Business Management*. Harcourt Brace Janovich, 1989.

Holtz, Herman. *How to Make Money With Your Desktop Computer*. Wiley, 1989.

Holtz, Herman. *How to Make Money with Your Micro*. Wiley, 1989.

Hopfenmuller, Steven A. *Fringe Benefits Guidebook for Small Businesses*. Hooksett Publishing, 1987.

Hubbard, Brian. *Entrepreneurs & Inventors Annual*. In-Time Publications, 1988.

Hull, Christopher; Hiern, Benny; Storey, David-Editor. *Helping Small Firms Grow: An Implementation Approach*. Routledge Chapman & Hall, 1988.

J. K. Lasser Tax Institute Staff. *How to Run a Small Business*. McGraw, 1989.

J. K. Lasser Tax Institute Staff; Spicer & Oppenheim Staff. *J. K. Lasser's Tax Guide for the Small Business 1989*. Prentice Hall, 1989.

Kingstone, Brett. *Student Entrepreneur's Guide: How to Start and Run Your Own Business*. McGraw, 1989.

Krupa, Arlene; Kirk-Kuwaye, Chris. *Couplepower: How to be Partners in Love and Business*. Dodd, 1988.

Kuehl, Charles; Lambing, Peggy. *Small Business: Planning & Management*. Dryden Press, 1989.

Kuriloff, Arthur H.; Hemphill, John M. *Starting & Managing the Small Business*. McGraw, 1988.

Laventhol; Horwath. *Leventhol & Horwath's Small Business Tax Preparation Guide*. Bantam, 1987.

Lester, Mary. *A Woman's Guide to Starting a Small Business*. Pilot Books, 1989.

Levitt, Mortimer. *How to Start Your Own Business Without Losing Your Shirt: Secrets of the Artful Entrepreneur*. Macmillan, 1988.

Lloyd, Bruce-Editor. *Entrepreneurship: Creating & Managing New Ventures*. Pergamon, 1989.

MacPhee, Wiliam. *Rare Breed: The Entrepreneur, An American Culture*. Probus Publishing Company, 1987.

Mancuso, Joseph R. *Mancuso's Small Business Resource Guide 1988–89*. Prentice Hall, 1988.

Megginson, Leon C.; Scott, Charles R.; Trueblood, Lyle R.; Megginson, William C. *Successful Small Business Management*. Irwin, 1988.

Metcalfe, J. S.-Editor; Barber, J.-Editor; Porteous, M.-Editor. *The Barriers to Growth in Small Firms*. Routledge Chapman & Hall, 1989.

O'Donnell, Kildulf. *Entrepreneur Kit: The Marketing Plan*. Lord Publishing, 1988.

Parson, Mary J. *Managing the One-Person Business*. Dodd, 1988.

Penderghast, Thomas F. *Entrepreneurial Simulation Program*. Harcourt Brace Janovich, 1988.

Perry, Larry, L. *Small Business Audit Manual*. Prentice Hall, 1987.

Riolo, Al; Greenberg, Ellen. *The New-Idea Success Book: Starting a Money-Making Business*. TAB BOOKS, 1988.

Ronstadt, Robert C. *Entrepreneur Kit: Feasibility Plan*. Lord Publishing, 1988.

Ronstadt, Robert C. *Entrepreneurial Finance: Taking Control of Your Financial Decision Making*. Lord Publishing, 1988.

Ryans, Cynthia C. *Managing the Small Business: Insights & Readings*. Prentice Hall, 1989.

Scarborough, Norman M.; Zimmerer, Thomas W. *Effective Small Business Management*. Merrill, 1988.

Schollhammer, Hans; Kuriloff, Arthur H. *Entrepreneurship & Small Business Management*. Krieger, 1988.

Smith, Albert C., Jr.; Smith, Albert, III-Editor. *Little Guy's Business Success Guide*. Cromwell-Smith, 1988.

Solomon, Mel. *Basics You Should Know Before Starting your Own Business*. Vantage, 1988.

Steinhoff, Daniel; Burgess, John. *Small Business Management Fundamentals*. McGraw, 1988.

Stevens, Mark. *The Macmillan Small Business Handbook*. Macmillan, 1988.

Strobel. *S Corporations Tax & Business Manual*. Wiley, 1988.

Timmons, Jeffry, A. *New Business Opportunities: Getting to the Right Place at the Right Time.* Brick House Publishing, 1990.

Timmons, Jeffry A. *The Entrepreneurial Mind.* Brick House Publishing, 1989.

Walker, Charles L. *Evaluation & Management Guide or the Small Business Ventures.* Carlton, 1988.

Walters, Kenneth-Editor. *Entrepreneurial Management: New Technology & New Market Development.* Ballinger Publishing, 1988.

Weintz, Walter H. *The Solid Gold Mailbox: How to Create Winning Mail Order Campaigns by One Who's Done It All.* Wiley, 1987.

Woy, Patricia A. *Small Businesses That Grow & Grow & Grow.* Betterway Publications, 1989.

Zimmerer, Thomas W.; Scarborough, Norman. *Small Business Fundamentals.* Merrill, 1988.

Zuckerman, Laurie B. *On Your Own: A Woman's Guide to Building a Business.* Upstart Publishing, 1989.

Advertising and forms of business ownership

Aaker, David A.; Myers, John G. *Advertising Management.* Prentice Hall, 1987.

Batra, Rajeev-Editor; Glazer, Rashi-Editor. *Cable TV Advertising: In Search of the Right Formula.* Greenwood, 1989.

Berkman, Harold W.; Gilson, Christopher. *Advertising: Concepts & Strategies.* McGraw, 1987.

Borgman, Harry. *Advertising Layout Techniques.* Watson-Guptill, 1988.

Bovee, Arens. *Contemporary Advertising.* Irwin, 1988.

Cooper. *How to Price a Business: A Handbook for Sellers & Buyers & Their Accountants, Appraisers, Attorneys, Banker.* Wiley, 1988.

Dunn, Watson S.; Barban, Arnold; Krugman, Dean; Reid, Len. *Advertising: Its Role in Modern Marketing.* Dryden Press, 1989.

Farris, Paul W.; Quelch, John A. *Advertising & Promotion Management.* Krieger, 1987.

Fueroghne, Dean K. *But the People in Legal Said . . . : A Guide to Current Legal Issues in Advertising.* Dow Jones-Irwin, 1988.

Greyser. *Cases in Advertising Communication Management.* Prentice Hall, 1990.

How to Get the Best Advertising Buys. Gordon Press, 1987.

Jones, John P. *Does It Pay to Advertise?: Cases Illustrating Successful Brand Advertising.* Lexington Books, 1989.

Jewler, A. Jerome. *Creative Strategy in Advertising.* Wadsworth Publishing, 1989.

Lindsey, Jennifer. *Joint Ventures & Corporate Partnerships: A Step-by-Step Guide to Forming Strategic Business Alliances.* Probus Publishing Company, 1989.

Marglin, Stephen A. *Growth, Distribution, & Prices.* Harvard University Press, 1987.

Marra, James L. *Advertising Creativity.* Prentice Hall, 1989.

McGann, Anthony F.; Russell, John T. *Advertising Media: A Managerial Approach.* Irwin, 1987.

Meeske, Milan D.; Norris, R. C. *Copywriting for the Electronic Media: A Practical Guide*. Wadsworth Publishing, 1987.

Miles, Raymond C. *How to Price a Business: A Buyers & Sellers Guide*. Prentice Hall, 1988.

Mini-Clip Art for Small Space Ads. Gordon Press, 1987.

Mohn, Reinhard. *Success Through Partnership*. Doubleday, 1988.

Norris, James. *Advertising*. Prentice Hall, 1989.

Patti, Charles H.; Frazer, Charles F. *Advertising: A Decision-Making Approach*. Dryden Press, 1988.

Pratt, James. *Corporate, Partnership, Estate & Gift Taxation: 1990 Edition*. Irwin, 1989.

Prentice Hall Editorial Staff. *Partnership Tax Handbook*. Prentice Hall, 1989.

Priemer, August B. *Effective Media Planning: A Guide to Help Advertisers & Agencies Develop Plans That Work*. Lexington Books, 1989.

Quelch, John A.; Farris, Paul W. *Cases in Advertising & Promotion Management*. Irwin, 1987.

Russell, J. Thomas; Verrill, Glen; Lane, Ron. *Kleppner's Advertising Procedure*. Prentice Hall, 1988.

Salz, Nancy L. *How to Get the Best Advertising from Your Agency: How It Works, How to Work with It - A Management Primer for Advertisers*. Dow Jones-Irwin, 1988.

Schlemmer, Richard M. *Handbook of Advertising Art Production*. Prentice Hall, 1990.

Semon, Larry. *Did You See My Ad?* Brick House Publishing, 1988.

Seymour, Daniel T.-Editor. *The Pricing Decision: A Strategic Planner for Marketing Professionals*. Probus Publishing Company, 1988.

Smith, Cynthia S. *How to Get Big Results from a Small Advertising Budget*. Carol Publishing Group, 1989.

Viladas, Luisa. *Advertising That Pays for Itself*. Havemeyer Books, 1987.

Wagner, W.F. *Advertising in the Yellow Pages: How to Boost Profits & Avoid Pitfalls*. Harvest Press LA, 1987.

Wells, William; Burnett, John; Moriarty, Sandra. *Advertising: Principles & Practice*. Prentice Hall, 1989.

White, Roderick. *Advertising*. McGraw, 1989.

Business plans

Bangs, David H., Jr. *The Business Planning Guide: Creating a Plan for Success in Your Own Business*. Upstart Publishing, 1989.

Fallek, Max; Phelps, Sara-Illustrator. *How to Write Your Own Business Plan Project Kit*. American Institute of Small Business, 1989.

Career change

Asseng, Nathan. *Midstream Changes: People Who Started Over & Made It Work*. Lerner Publications, 1989.

Caple, John. *The Right Work: Finding It & Making It Right*. Dodd, 1987.

Cetron, Marvin; Davies, Owen. *The Great Job Shakeout of the 1990s: All You'll Ever Need to Find the Great Jobs of the Future*. S&S, 1988.

Dawson, Kenneth M.; Dawson, Sheryl N. *Job Search: The Total System*. Dawson & Dawson, 1988.

Fox, Marcia R. *Put Your Degree to Work: The New Professional's Guide to Career Planning & Job Hunting*. Norton, 1988.

Fritz, Roger. *Nobody Gets Rich Working for Somebody Else*. Dodd, 1987.

Halloran, James W. *The Right Fit: The Entrepreneur's Guide to Finding the Perfect Business*. TAB BOOKS, 1988.

How Do I Find the Right Job?: Read This Book. Wiley, 1989.

Levinson, Jay C. *Quit Your Job!* Dodd, 1987.

Madry, B.R. *Job Seekers Guide*. Milady Publishing, 1987.

Nakell, Mark; Meyers, Steven-Illustrator. *The Complete Job Sight Program*. Kit Group, 1987.

Silliphant, Leigh; Silliphant Sureleigh. *Making Seventy Thousand Dollars a Year as a Self-Employed Manufacturer's Representative*. Ten Speed Press, 1988.

Strasser, Stephen; Sena, John. *Transitions: Successfully Managing Changes in Your Career*. Prentice Hall, 1989.

Waxler, Myer; Wolf, Robert L. *Goodbye Job, Hello Me: Self-Discovery Through Self-Employment*. Scott F, 1987.

Weinberg, Janice. *How to Win the Job You Really Want*. H Holt & Company, 1989.

Zey, Michael. *The Right Move: How to Find the Perfect Job*. Ballantine, 1988.

Customer service

Kausen, Robert. *Customer Satisfaction Guaranteed: A New Approach to Customer Service, Bedside Manner, & Relationship Ease*. Life Education, 1989.

Poppe, Fred C. *Fifty Rules to Keep a Client Happy*. Harper Row, 1988.

Display and store design

Kitsukana, Shin. *European Window Displays*. Rockport Publications, 1987.

Mikoda, Naoki. *Store & Sign Design*. Rockport Publications, 1988.

Shotenkenchiku-sha-Editor. *European Shop Designs*. Rockport Publications, 1987.

Wrigley, Neil-Editor. *Store Choice, Store Location & Market Analysis*. Routledge Chapman & Hall, 1988.

Employees

Herzberg, F.; Mausner, B.; Peterson, R.; Capwell, D.; Brief, Arthur P.-Editor. *Job Attitudes: Review of Research & Opinion*. Garland Publishing, 1987.

Lessem, Ronnie. *Entrepreneurship: Developing the Individual in Business*. Gower Publishing Company, 1987.

Levering, Robert. *A Great Place to Work: What Makes Some Employers So Good - & Most So Bad*. Random, 1988.

Slimmon, Robert F. *Successful Pension Design for Small to Medium-Sized Businesses*. Prentice Hall, 1987.

Financial management and accounting

Bangs, David H., Jr. *Cash Flow Control Guide*. Upstart Publications, 1987.

Brigham, Eugene; Gapenski, Louis. *Cases in Financial Management*. Dryden Press, 1989.

Brooks. *Financial Management Decision Game*. Irwin, 1987.

Butters, J. Keith-Editor; Fruhan, William E., Jr.-Editor; Mullins, David W.-Editor; Piper, Thomas R.-Editor. *Case Problems in Finance*. Irwin, 1987.

Cooley, Philip. *Advances in Business Financial Management*. Dryden Press, 1989.

Cooley, Philip L.; Roden, Peyton F. *Business Financial Management*. Dryden Press, 1988.

Davidoff, Doris; Davidoff, Philip G. *Financial Management for Travel Agencies*. Delmar, 1987.

Hampton, John J. *Financial Decision Making: Concepts, Problems & Cases*. Prentice Hall, 1989.

Harrington, Diana R. *Case Studies in Financial Decision Making*. Dryden Press, 1988.

Analysis. Dow Jones Irwin, 1989.

Harrington, Wilson. *Corporate Financial Analysis*. Irwin, 1989.

Heyman, H.G.; Bloom, Robert. *Decision Support Systems in Finance & Accounting*. Greenwood, 1988.

Kelsay, Susan M.-Editor. *Annual Statement Studies*. Robert Morris Associates, 1989.

Marsh, William; Kuniansky, Harry. *Case Problems in Financial Management*. Prentice Hall, 1988.

Mayo, Herbert B. *Finance: An Introduction*. Dryden Press, 1988.

Minars, David. *Business Startups: The Professional's Guide to Tax & Financial Strategies*. Prentice Hall, 1987.

Ratner, Ellis-Editor; Coler, Mark-Editor. *Financial Services: The Expert's Guide*. Prentice Hall, 1987.

Ross, Stephan; Westerfield, Randy. *Corporate Finance*. Irwin, 1989.

Scott, David; Keown, Arthur J.; Petty, J. William; Martin, John D. *Basic Financial Management*. Prentice Hall, 1988.

Shim. Jae K.; Siegel, Joel G. *Handbook of Financial Analysis, Forecasting & Modeling*. Prentice Hall, 1987.

Siegel, Joel G.; Shim, Jae K. *Encyclopedic Dictionary of Accounting & Finance*. Prentice Hall, 1989.

Sorter, George H.; Ingberman, Monroe; Maximon, Hillel M. *Financial Accounting: Events & Cash Flow Approach*. McGraw, 1989.

Troy, Leo. *Almanac of Business & Industrial Financial Ratios: 1989 Edition*. Prentice Hall, 1989.

Turock, Betty; Schuman, Patricia G.-Frwd. by. *Creating a Financial Plan*. Neal-Schuman, 1990.

Vale, Philip. *Financial Management Handbook*. Gower Publishing Company, 1987.

Van Horne, James C. *Financial Management & Policy*. Prentice Hall, 1989.

Viscione, Jerry A.; Roberts, Gordon. *Contemporary Financial Management*. Merrill, 1987.

Financing and funding

Blum, Laurie. *Free Money: For Small Business & Entrepreneurs*. Wiley, 1989.

Goldstein, Arnold S. *How to Buy a Great Business with No Cash Down*. Wiley, 1989.

Haines, Lionel. *How to Buy a Business with Little or None of Your Own Money: The ABC's of Leveraged Buy-outs*. Times Books, 1987.

Mangold, M. A. *How to Buy a Small Business*. Pilot Books, 1987.

Rhyne, Elisabeth H. *Small Business, Banks, & SBA Loan Guarantees: Subsidizing the Weak or Bridging a Credit Gap?* Greenwood, 1988.

Senn, Mark A. *Commercial Real Estate Leases: Preparation & Negotiation. 1989 Cumulative Supplement*. Wiley, 1989.

Marketing and promotion (also see advertising)

Breen, George; Blankenship, A. B. *Do-It-Yourself Marketing Research*. McGraw, 1989.

Burnett, Ed. *The Complete Direct Mail List Handbook: Everything You Need to Know About Lists & How to Use Them for Greater Profit*. Prentice Hall, 1988.

MARDEV Limited Staff-Editor. *Direct Mail Databook*. Gower Publishing Company, 1987.

Pfeiffer, William S. *Proposal Writing: The Art of Friendly Persuasion*. Merril, 1988.

Retzler, Kathryn. *Direct Marketing: The Proven Path to Successful Sales*. Scott F, 1988.

Roberts, Mary L.; Berger, Paul. *Direct Marketing Management*. Prentice Hall, 1989.

Index